01/06

White House Nannies

WHITE HOUSE
NANNIES

BARBARA KLINE

JEREMY P. TARCHER/PENGUIN

a member of Penguin Group (USA) Inc.

NEW YORK

JEREMY P. TARCHER/PENGUIN
Published by the Penguin Group
Penguin Group (USA) Inc., 375 Hudson Street, New York, New York 10014, USA •
Penguin Group (Canada), 10 Alcorn Avenue, Toronto, Ontario M4V 3B2, Canada
(a division of Pearson Penguin Canada Inc.) • Penguin Books Ltd, 80 Strand, London
WC2R 0RL, England • Penguin Ireland, 25 St Stephen's Green, Dublin 2, Ireland
(a division of Penguin Books Ltd) • Penguin Group (Australia), 250 Camberwell
Road, Camberwell, Victoria 3124, Australia (a division of Pearson Australia Group
Pty Ltd) • Penguin Books India Pvt Ltd, 11 Community Centre, Panchsheel Park,
New Delhi–110 017, India • Penguin Group (NZ), Cnr Airborne and Rosedale
Roads, Albany, Auckland 1310, New Zealand (a division of Pearson New Zealand
Ltd) • Penguin Books (South Africa) (Pty) Ltd, 24 Sturdee Avenue, Rosebank,
Johannesburg 2196, South Africa • Penguin Books Ltd, Registered Offices:
80 Strand, London WC2R 0RL, England

Most Tarcher/Penguin books are available at special quantity discounts for bulk
purchase for sales promotions, premiums, fund-raising, and educational needs.
Special books or book excerpts also can be created to fit specific needs.
For details, write Penguin Group (USA) Inc. Special Markets,
375 Hudson Street, New York, NY 10014.

Library of Congress Cataloging-in-Publication Data

Kline, Barbara, date.
White House Nannies / Barbara Kline.
p. cm.
ISBN 1-58542-410-2
1. Kline, Barbara. 2. White House Nannies (Firm). 3. Nanny placement
agencies—Washington (D.C.)—Anecdotes. 4. Nannies—Washington (D.C.)—
Anecdotes. 5. Child care—Washington (D.C.)—Anecdotes. 6. Elite (Social
sciences)—Washington (D.C.)—Anecdotes. I. Title.

HQ778.67.W36K58   2005   2004060222
649'.092—dc22

Printed in the United States of America
1   3   5   7   9   10   8   6   4   2

This book is printed on acid-free paper. ∞

BOOK DESIGN BY AMANDA DEWEY

The names and identifying characteristics of most real people described in this book
have been changed to protect the privacy of the individuals involved. Other
people who appear in the book are entirely fictional characters.

In memory of my mother, Bernice R. Goldstein

For Richard, Matt, and Gillian

The precise intersection of many women's most passionate impulses—their profound, almost physical love for their children and their fervent wish to make something of themselves beyond their own doorstep—is the exact spot where nannies show up for work each day.

—CAITLIN FLANAGAN, "How Serfdom Saved the Women's Movement: Dispatches from the Nanny Wars," *The Atlantic Monthly*, March 2004

THE MIRACLE OF
MOTHERHOOD

July, 1983

After eight years of scooping ice cream on Capitol Hill, one night I found myself on the floor of the Ice Cream Lobby with a gun aimed at my head. Clearly I needed to find a new profession—not to mention, someone to take care of my baby while I looked for one.

I wasn't a great stay-at-home mother—even if we could have afforded it. My adorable son, Matthew, was as high maintenance as babies come. He was a good eater, a lousy sleeper, and the rest of the time, he howled. Even though I was an intelligent thirty-three-year-old, I couldn't get through the day alone with my child without feeling like a failure. The miracle of motherhood, I began to think, is that more of us don't run away from home.

How can seven pounds bring such joy—and cause such chaos? After running my own successful business for years while my husband, Richard, worked in real estate, we assumed we were up to the task of parenting. How tough could it be for two competent adults plus a regular babysitter to handle one baby?

But I made every mistake in the *Hiring Childcare* book; we went through so many neighborhood sitters, we couldn't keep their names straight. Marva couldn't navigate public transportation and get to work on time. Connie, it turned out, didn't like babies. Then I called Washington's Most Reputable Nanny Agency. They sent me Lucille, who walked in each morning, made herself a fried egg sandwich, and read my *Washington Post* while I tried to keep Matt from screaming and disturbing her breakfast.

When you're desperate for twelve seconds alone in the bathroom, you'll hire almost anyone—which seemed to be that nanny agency's philosophy.

Two working parents plus a child in diapers minus reliable childcare equals hysteria. Children need a village, or at least an extended family. Mine was far away, and all our friends were in the same dire straits. I launched a self-serving experiment to solve our common problem.

White House Nannies has been liberating Washington parents—myself included—ever since. Who knew that my brainchild would take off like a toddler with a dangerous object? And that helping these parents keep their jobs and families from crashing on a daily basis would be so much fun? These fascinating Washingtonians—Cabinet members and network nabobs—and their amazing variety of nannies have kept me and my staff laughing for the past twenty years.

(You'll hear about the bad days later.)

. . .

I'm a big talker, but I've become an even better listener. I ask clients and prospective nannies the right questions and I pay attention to what they say. My fact-finding skills are so good by now that some references want to know if I work for the FBI. And after I've matched a nanny to a family, there's "follow-up" and even occasional fallout. This means I function as an amateur therapist, mediator, labor contract attorney, pediatrician, child behavior specialist, and even private-school consultant. If only I could bill by the hour at my attorney-clients' rates.

Finding great jobs for women from all over the globe has taught me how lucky any mother is who doesn't have to leave her children and travel thousands of miles to take care of someone else's. *Do you have any British nannies?* I hear all the time. Or *Do you have someone from Latin America?* I tell these clients what I've learned: Wonderful nannies come from every country, even from some I've never heard of.

My husband manages the financial side of the business and occasionally helps out with the amazing variety of requests we get for temporary nannies. Out-of-town attorneys arguing cases before the Supreme Court need someone to watch their children at the hotel, and Inauguration guests need invisible children while they're in town. An opera singer once needed someone to watch her newborn while she sang at the Kennedy Center, and another hotel guest wanted one-on-one care for—I kid you not—his Chihuahua!

The best thing about my business is the novelty of every day:

new clients, children, and nannies; new interpersonal quirks and logistics to smooth out. Whatever your childcare issues are—and everyone has *some*—I'm an inveterate optimist, always ready to solve the next dilemma.

Some days I do. And when I don't, at least I get a good story out of the deal.

Here are many of my favorites.

WHITE HOUSE NANNIES

1.

THE BIGGEST SECRET
IN WASHINGTON

N O ONE MOVES to Washington to kick back. The most
driven, educated workforce in the nation is here, for government or international trade or lobbying, for high-
tech or telecom—what's left of it. No one is here to do lunch or
play golf. They're here to compete with the rest of their elite tribe,
all those valedictorians, class presidents, and law review editors,
voted just as likely to succeed as they were.

Whatever their game, many of these Extremely Important
Players won't be here long. Sooner or later, the District's infamous revolving door will probably eject them back *out there*
again, to the place they came from. Just so they remember that
D.C. isn't the *only* center of the universe.

Most of my clients are in their potent prime, between
twenty-eight and forty-four years old and on Marriage Number
One. They work harder than anyone outside the Beltway—or so

they think. Scrambling to the top of whatever game they play means no downtime.

And then, in the middle of these lives already crammed with crucial obligations, they have babies. Extended families live far away, so these power-elite couples try to keep the government running without the luxury of any free backup at home.

The highest percentage of families with in-home childcare live right here (11 percent compared to a 5.3 percent national average). They log more air miles, meetings, and fifteen-hour workdays than most of us can imagine. Now these parents know what tired really is.

Husbands help, of course. But everyone knows where the parenting buck stops—after the nanny goes off duty. Don't forget, we have hardly any doting grandparents, aunts, and uncles to share the joy and pitch in when there's an emergency.

This is where I come in—to dispatch a miraculous savior to the suddenly chaotic, childcentric home of a congressperson, media mogul, or federal judge. One of my White House Nannies will calm the tantrum and handle the calamity they never in a million years expected—especially not when all hell is breaking loose in the national, international, or interplanetary arena.

If you've already called me, the crisis a few miles away will be over before you're out of your West Wing meeting or back from Asia. No matter how many hours you spend away from your home and family, when you finally get back there, life will be harmonious—because you have a White House Nanny.

And even if this isn't *always* the case, my batting average is still pretty good.

So I think of myself as the *other* chief of Homeland Security.

. . .

My hometown is really another kind of Hollywood—just as overpopulated with high-profile celebrities who consider themselves the most entitled citizens in the universe. L.A. super-stars may wear glitzy, shocking outfits while D.C. men and women only get as crazy as seersucker suits and maybe a designer shirt and tie. But you can follow the moves and moods of *our* stars too—on C-SPAN, Leno, or *Aljazeera.*

We make the news, whether you see it on television or the web, in the *Wall Street Journal, Newsweek,* or the tabloids. HILL'S SEX DIARIST REVEALS ALL I read in this morning's paper about a young staffer, a "Washingtonienne," who wrote—on a Senate office computer—all about her lunch-hour trysts with politicos.

She lost her job, but she got a terrific book deal.

So nature and lust eventually blow our power couples way off course, into the all-consuming underground activity known as Having a Family. But you might never know that, because even the most visible Washingtonians keep their offspring behind closed doors. Hidden from the media.

This is the major difference between *Bel Air* and Bethesda: Hollywood parents consider even their unborn children public relations *gold.* (Remember naked, about-to-deliver Demi Moore on the cover of *Vanity Fair*?) Entertainment celebrities appear in the limelight with their designer-dressed darlings whenever they get the chance. Just check out any issue of *People* magazine: Johnny Depp says he'd like a hundred children, Madonna may be with child again, and Gwyneth Paltrow's parading her baby daughter, Apple, everywhere.

But here in D.C., our stars protect their children from public scrutiny. A toddler tantrum can ruin a congressperson's image faster than a Gallup poll can plummet. Between terrorism and the federal budget, my clients have enough of the Unpredictable to deal with, and, big news: *Children aren't controllable.* They need to be contained and trained by the right nanny, preferably way off-stage. In case they do something *embarrassing.*

Unless, of course, it's an election year, when politicians suddenly parade offspring *everywhere,* the stars of their campaigns. The only other time these political children are in the media is when they dress inappropriately for a state occasion. Or when they're thrown out of prep school for using drugs, or arrested for drunk driving.

It isn't true that politicians kiss everyone's babies but their own, although you might get that impression: The real goings-on with their children are their Deep Throat secrets.

But when my phone rings, these children are not the first thing I hear about.

"I'm so glad I found your agency. This is the Commissioner." *The actual Commish?* Or, "I'm the CEO of, the Chief Prosecutor of, the President of, the Chairman of, the Governor of, the Prosecutor of—" ad infinitum. Next come the acronyms, so numerous they're humorous; even though they multiply daily like bacteria. Along with all the familiar ones such as the DOD, FTC, and USAID, I'm expected to know what dozens of others stand for, such as the CCPCJ (Commission on Crime Prevention and Criminal Justice) and the IBWM (International Bureau of Weights and Measures). And, of course, be duly impressed.

This is a *titled* town, and no one introduces him- or herself without their entire résumé to back them up. Over the years, I've talked to a governor of the Federal Reserve, a solicitor general, and a comptroller of the currency, so I'm used to it. I wait patiently, filing my nails and organizing my papers while they tell me where they work, how huge their responsibilities are, and how much they have to travel. Then I hear all about their even busier, more important husbands (or wives).

Finally my prospective clients mention their extracurricular activities: eight-year-old brilliant twins, a four-year-old gymnast, and a brand-new baby girl who can already sing on key.

"Jessica is two and needs companionship."

"Gregory adores baseball, and of course by the time we get home it's too dark to play."

"I love my children."

"I have to get back to my *life*."

Their careers are on track, but their home lives are derailing and I get to hear their not-so-silent screams for help.

"How do I make this work?"

Easy. You've already taken the right first step and called me.

2.

CLOSETGATE

THE SECRETARY RINGS the phone through to my desk exactly four seconds after the digital clock has flashed 9:00 A.M. on a Monday morning in August. When I shout out "Four seconds," my assistant, Karen, laughs. It's the call no one wants to take. Something bad has happened over the weekend, and someone can't wait to tell us about it.

I'm not alarmed when they call at 9:10 or even 9:05. But when the phone rings the instant we click off the answering machine, a parent has been pacing for hours, desperately waiting to call.

And desperation is our raison d'être.

If I placed bets about these calls, I'd be rich: Either a nanny has quit or she's been fired. Occasionally, and most heinous of all, she's been "nanny-napped" by a conniving, equally desperate, Washington parent. But no matter why the nanny is gone, somewhere in an elegant, tree-lined enclave of elected officials, media stars, and attorneys, behind a VIP's securely closed door, *hell has broken loose.*

I recognize the resonant, commanding voice before I hear her name because I see Janette Huntington all the time on network news. ABC, CBS, NBC, the initials don't really matter. When Janette's the stunning White House correspondent, you pay attention. And ever since she started *showing* on camera, her high-profile pregnancy has been big news.

Our superstar will probably visit motherhood long enough to do an eyewitness report as if it's just another assignment. She'll be back on the air so soon after giving birth, we'll barely have missed her. I'm sure Huntington didn't wait until now to find the perfect caregiver, so the nanny she lined up ages ago must have vanished. Now, along with 9/11, Afghanistan, and the reeling economy, Janette has a calamity of her own to report.

"My baby's due in twenty-nine days and my nanny just backed out!" she tells me, her calm efficiency hardly masking her hysteria. The newswoman I saw with the President in the World Trade "pit" has turned into any distraught working woman in her last trimester whose childcare arrangements have fallen apart. She's hovering between abject despair and panic attack, firing information at me faster than the News at Eleven.

Pre-first-baby angst isn't unusual, of course. But in this case, you'd think the sky was falling. *I did everything right. How could such a crisis happen to* me?

"Elizabeth was so excited about working for us," Janette tells me. It seems that the nanny decided, at the very last minute, that her prospective quarters didn't have enough closet space.

"How disappointing." I sympathize, ready to move on.

But Janette is still struggling with this terrible news. "I can't believe she chose someone else's baby over mine," she whimpers. The cool, restrained reporter is so irrational she's decided that her soon-to-be-award-winning child was *rejected*. In utero. Some underling had the unmitigated gall to choose another baby over hers!

The nanny-to-be must have gone on a shopping spree and realized she needed more space for all those new outfits. *It wouldn't hurt to go out on a few more exploratory interviews,* she figured. After that, she was as good as gone. Anyone sane knows it's absurd to give up a great job because your wardrobe might be a bit squashed. But after working with ego-driven clients, often-unrealistic clients—*and* their equally unrealistic help—the closet story doesn't surprise me.

News Celeb on the Edge would be a good title for my documentary about Controllers Who Lose Control. Like most of my clients, Janette probably started networking her childcare options even before she was pregnant. Her rare stroke of bad luck is the first clue that her power has mysteriously evaporated. This helplessness comes with the parenting territory.

I've figured out how to succeed in this competitive town, many Washington mothers assume. *I can certainly find my own nanny.* And a lot of them try. Some parents are in Human Resources and hire large staffs for government agencies or private-sector corporations. *How hard could it be to find my own childcare?*

But when the nanny they find on their own turns out to be inexperienced, a *terrible* fit, or not exactly legal (just like pregnancy, you are or you aren't), they call me.

Like so many others, Janette conducted exhaustive first-trimester interviews with several nannies, then put the very best one "on reserve." It's a classic case: the comeuppance of the superachievers. My clients are highly competent at what they do and connected enough to pull any string in town, but that doesn't mean they should do my job. Even though Janette broke that rule, now I know her as a mother in distress, and I like her right away. She's outraged, but she's totally *real*.

"I represent a very prominent family," someone's assistant said at the end of a busy Friday, pretension dripping off his every word.

"Aren't they all?" I answered, my tact already turned off for the weekend. The caller identified himself as the *Chief of Staff* for, indeed, a prominent socialite who gives generously to Washington institutions.

Most Washington parents with impressive titles are smart enough to call me themselves. When someone calls me about their boss's childcare, I see a red flag. And when I hear "Chief of Staff," I immediately think White House—West Wing.

"I'd really like to speak to the child's mother," I said. The boss would definitely call, but she never had the time. Eventually, I found out what I could about the position from the underling and chose a nanny for the six-year-old boy and his apparently hands-off parents.

The nanny and I met Mr. Chief of Staff for high tea at the Ritz-Carlton, where the interview went so well that I optimistically picked up the tab. The nanny was then taken home to meet the invisible employers.

"You've hit the ball out of the park," I heard, again second-hand. "The young lady is perfect. My boss will call to finalize the arrangements."

But I never heard from her, and I have no idea why. Was the nanny asking for too high a salary? Was the child abducted and held for ransom? If I'd followed my own rule—*talk to the principal*—I'd have known what went wrong. That was one high tea I was sorry I paid for.

Janette's smart enough to make her own phone calls, but by hiring a nanny six months before her due date, she'd given the young woman too much time to look for something even better. I'm sure the Huntington-Wilder nanny suite is as wonderful as it sounds: bedroom, sitting room, large bathroom; a private entrance in a beautiful bucolic Spring Valley home, where there is no other kind. But that nanny wanted a big closet, and one was bound to come along.

"She asked if she could store some of her things in the playroom," Janette tells me. "But my parents already sent us one of those Baby Einstein play gyms, and I know there'll be a lot more toys soon, so we really want to keep that space for the baby."

I've doodled *lousy closet* on my legal pad. If it torpedoed one deal, it'll torpedo another one, unless I'm careful.

Whenever I check out a nanny's quarters, I always ask myself if I'd want to put my daughter there. I've had to deliver the bad news that a windowless room in the basement of a gorgeous 10,000-square-foot Potomac house is against code. I've seen furnaces in the nanny's closet, and bathrooms that double as laundry rooms.

On the other end of the spectrum, I've seen nanny suites with separate kitchens and space to entertain friends. One couple actually purchased a condominium for their nanny, down the hall from their own apartment in a luxury downtown high-rise. I've seen ninety-five-dollar-a-yard chintz-upholstered sofas and matching wallpaper.

I keep discovering new deal-breakers to watch out for. One young woman wants a swimming pool; another refuses to iron the children's party clothes. A nanny's boyfriend might convince her not to live with the "snobs in Potomac" since he has a perfectly good double-wide outside D.C.

Janette is yet another important Washingtonian to find out that as soon as she conceived, all bets were off. Once you've signed up for parenthood, nothing else is sacred—not network crises, summit meetings, Senate bills, or romantic dinners. In this town, earaches, toddler tantrums, and nanny mood swings feel like national emergencies.

"I called Elizabeth several times and left messages about getting together to go over details," Janette reports. My clients are accustomed to managing situations instead of getting stuck in them, so they tend to analyze what went wrong. I'd like to move forward, but Janette's saga continues. The nanny wasn't returning her calls, but she was in pre-motherhood denial and had no idea trouble was brewing.

She finally took Elizabeth—from upper-crust Grosse Pointe, Michigan, by the way—to a swanky seventy-five-dollar tea at the Tyson's Corner Ritz-Carlton. Instead of meeting at Starbucks, Janette thought they should chat in a properly formal, lavish setting. "You know, to send the right signal. You've been to the Tyson's Ritz, haven't you?" she asks. "I wanted our nanny to know there will be special treats if things go well."

She's sure I'll agree that any nanny would jump at such extravagance. Nanny-bribing is common, often in the form of a "signing bonus," which can exceed a thousand dollars. Sometimes a "nanny car" is part of the bargain. A recent client who owned a luxury-car dealership actually promised his nanny that if she stayed five years, the car would be hers.

I already like Janette for her earnestness, but when she uses the word "treats," I think of a snooty dog trainer offering bits of dried liver to a performing poodle. She's not my first client to consider her nanny somewhere between a pet and an invisible life form.

"Do you believe she didn't even have the decency to tell me *before* we sat down?" Of course I do—I'm used to it. Nothing, certainly not Earl Grey and crumpets, could have changed Janette's fate.

"That goddamned closet is *eight feet long.*" She's so flabbergasted about the betrayal that she even lets her vocabulary slip. "I interviewed a family in Guatemala who live in a *house* smaller than that!" As if living conditions in Latin America have anything to do with the accommodations Washington nannies expect these days.

I find out eventually that the closet in question measures only two feet deep. And, by the way, this isn't Guatemala.

Not even a high salary or the promise of a Caribbean vacation had changed the nanny's mind. And when Janette finally offered her even more money, the nanny with the enormous wardrobe looked at her with pity.

While it happens to be about closets this time, nannies back out at the last moment for lots of reasons. Janette still wants to analyze what went wrong, but we don't have time. I interrupt her with the magic words: *I think I can help you.* There's hope, which calms her down so we can get to work.

Each time a Washington hotshot parent or parent-to-be calls me in distress, I witness this collision with reality. No matter what's going on in education or with the economy, Janette's top story right now is Nanny Anarchy.

Power-elite jobs don't have mommy tracks, and my clients usually need to be back at work full-time four to eight weeks after their child is born. Even that month or two isn't truly maternity *leave,* because they still have to be available for phone calls and whatever special projects their higher-ups request of them.

Bonding with one's newborn is considered an unnecessary indulgence in these circles. Media stars who don't accept this, or think they're the exception to the rule, will end up covering school-board meetings at some podunk network affiliate in Cleveland. Serious strivers like Janette and David have worked very hard to rise to the top of their games. All they're doing is having a baby. How can that change anything?

I'm Chairperson of some task force or other. My husband works for the Treasury. For AOL. For the Smithsonian. We're often out of town, and we both put in crazy hours. Oh, and we're pregnant.

By the way, Barbara, I run an empire.

How will you fit your child into your fascinating, already overburdened lives? I want to ask.

But don't, because I already know the answer: That will be the nanny's job.

Choate, Princeton, and Harvard Law have groomed Janette's husband, David Wilder, for his senior partnership in international litigation. As number two in his graduating class at Harvard, David has had his choice of positions at D.C.'s top firms.

After distinguishing herself summa cum laude at the University of Michigan, Janette went to the Medill School of Journalism at Northwestern on scholarship. After doing local reporting in San Francisco, she moved on to Atlanta, and then she was launched straight to the coveted White House Correspondent job in the *Capitol,* no surprise to anyone who knows how smart and driven Janette is. She's promised to be back on the air in a month looking as if she'd been to the Golden Door, instead of the way the rest of us look postpartum. Anyone in her business knows all you get is a maternity "burp."

Just as I'm going into a bit of a tailspin myself, my latest important client delivers some very good news. "Of course," she tells me in a scoffing tone, as if anyone who thinks otherwise is clueless, "We got the baby nurse right away, for three weeks. And thank *God* she had a free week after that." During one of David's board meetings, a partner who'd just returned to the firm after having her baby told him about an agency in New York that specializes in those legendary, minted-in-England baby nurses. Janette called right away and procured a professional with credentials named Mrs. Plumb.

The legend goes that when D.C. royals discover they're pregnant, *first* they call the baby nurse—and *then* they call their mother. I've met some couples who were so obsessed with doing things right they probably hired a baby nurse *and* a nanny while the sperm was still making its way north.

Enter the classic British perambulator-pushing baby nurse, a vanishing breed; she's the antidote to under-eye circles and post-pregnancy pudginess, soother of the maternal soul. Babies are *radioactive* to a broadcast career, and there will surely be newsroom plots to replace Janette with a younger, *non*-reproductive model. You can't even have a cold on the air, let alone a baby—even though this is like expecting an Olympic athlete not to break a sweat.

Janette has hired a secret weapon. Nurse Plumb will get her baby sleeping through the night and teach him or her aristocratic manners before leaving to rescue the next mother in distress. I've heard of parents who've called their baby nurse on her day off and put their screaming infants on the phone. *Is she hungry or over-*

tired? Do you think she has an earache? But the baby nurse has made it clear that she's off duty so they're on their own. After all, they're the *parents.*

Each baby nurse is a one-woman bodyguard, personal assistant, chef, and baby-whisperer. These experienced women in starched uniforms are often of advanced years, cloth diaper over one shoulder, sensible shoes, talcum-powder-scented pin-curled hair. This is their lifetime profession.

Most new parents, mere mortals, struggle through sleepless nights, endless diaper changes, and bottle-heatings. Privileged ones spend these precious days being pampered and resting peacefully. Baby is brought to his mother's bed to nurse at any hour, then whisked away to be walked and comforted through all-night crying bouts. One pays dearly for these services; the typical baby nurse fetches three hundred dollars or more per round-the-clock day. Baby nurses tend to smack of old money.

My mother had a registered nurse named Mrs. Woomer—I swear that was her name—old-fashioned, white starched uniform and cap. She coddled me and my sister and stayed with us for six years. And we were both lucky enough to have baby nurses for our own children. My sister's British baby nurse had worked for actual royalty, which she never let us forget. She was quintessentially Upper East Side, and she loved to parade my niece and nephew (who were swaddled in embroidered Porthault) through Central Park in their Rolls-Royce-like carriage.

The baby nurse I hired was more typical of Washington: less pretentious. Mrs. Boyce made my new journey seem a lot easier than it was going to be. Even though I didn't have to get back to work the way Janette does, I wouldn't have survived that excruciatingly difficult first month in the mother business without her. Mrs. Boyce was happy with my practical, basic baby carriage— more like a Volvo than my sister's Rolls-Royce version.

Janette and David's new arrival will be here in two weeks, more or less. With their impeccably credentialed baby nurse on board for a month, we've got six weeks to find and acclimate a nanny. If we're lucky, she'll be able to overlap with the baby nurse for a more comfortable transition.

An unexpected gap in Janette's schedule will wreak havoc on her ratings, so I have to get her back in action. Time to review my candidates and start the process rolling.

Otherwise, *I'll* end up stuck in an overdecorated nursery, rocking Janette's baby to sleep so she can race back to the studio.

Soon you'll understand why that's not a good idea.

3.

MOTHERS
WHO THINK

I start searching for the right person to send to the nanny-less Huntington-Wilders. It won't be hard to find someone so excited about the perks and prestige of this job that she'll overlook the skimpy storage space. At least that's what I *thought*—before I got Janette's fax: "Instead of filling out your application form, David and I thought our 'Prospective Nanny Letter' would be more helpful."

Janette Huntington-Wilder
1301 Wilton Road N.W.
Washington, D.C. 20016

Dear Prospective Nanny:
By this coming spring, February 15 to be exact, David and I will be first-time parents, and we're both so excited about this amazing new adventure.

To most efficiently determine the person best suited to care for our child, here are some general guidelines. Please send us this information so we can determine whom to interview. Because we both have highly demanding positions, we require the kind of vigilant, devoted care for our child that will provide us with absolute peace of mind.

We have prepared a contract for this position, with duties and expectations clearly spelled out, as well as compensation and vacation details.

Until our child is on a regulated feeding and sleeping schedule, we'll need your help on a 24-hour basis. You will be paid for between 50 and 75 hours of work per week, with Sundays off from noon until 9 P.M. You will be compensated for any additional hours at an overtime compensatory rate. We will hire an assistant nanny up to twice a month should that be necessary.

Because you will be sometimes spending more time with our baby than we'll be able to, we want to make sure you understand our parenting philosophy.

The television should never be on when our child is awake. His or her life should be filled with educational play, music, and reading. We've collected several books about childcare and the first year of life and expect you to consult them. Brain Building Games for Baby *and anything by T. Berry Brazelton are essential reading. We want our child to get lots of fresh air and exercise. Most important, we expect you to engage her or him and provide the warm, cheerful intellectual stimulation appropriate for the pre-verbal months.*

Kindly provide the following information:

1. *Tell us about your own childhood and family, including number of siblings and their birth order.*

2. What is your educational background? (Field of study and degrees, extracurricular activities in both high school and college)

3. List all previous employment as well as any experience relevant to a childcare position. Include names of employers and ages and gender of their children. Please provide us with telephone and e-mail contact information for at least three references.

4. Describe your approach to infant and early-childhood care. Do you think a baby should be allowed to cry in order to learn to comfort himself? How do you get babies on regular feeding, napping, and night sleeping schedules?

5. What is your approach to teaching language skills?

6. What are your personal television-viewing habits?

7. Are you willing to spend a lot of time outdoors regardless of weather?

8. Describe your feelings about discipline.

9. What are your social activities outside of work, and who are your primary friends? Are you married or in a serious relationship?

10. Where is your family and how often do you see one another?

11. What are your special skills and talents? Musical instruments? Languages? Dance or yoga training? Athletic strengths?

12. How long do you see yourself in our employ? Where do you want to be in five years?

Finally, please write 500 to 1,000 words telling us why you want this position.

I've spent twenty years refining the questions on my parents' application form, and each one helps me find the right person for the job. So it's *extremely irritating* when a first-time parent decides not to fill out my paperwork. But in this me-centered universe, sidestepping the rules is S.O.P. so I should be used to it.

"How will Baby ever see Mommy if he can't watch her on TV?" my assistant asks me. We know our media mothers. This one thinks she'll be able to micromanage her house and child by remote control, but I hope she'll lighten up with the right nanny.

But if Janette thinks great nannies grow on trees, she's laboring under a large misconception.

At least Janette and her husband are willing to pay the going rate: seven hundred dollars a week for the fifty-five-plus hours of help they'll need. Not every client wants to pay fair wages, especially Foreign Service, World Bank, and International Monetary Fund employees who've lived overseas. Clients who had ten (count 'em) docile servants do *everything* for them in Thailand are shocked to learn that one Washington nanny costs what they paid their entire staff in Bangkok.

"How will we manage?" one panicky mother asked. "We have two children. And they're at *Beauvoir*."

Her choices are my problem? She finally hired someone at ten dollars an hour, which she considered an insane amount of money. A few weeks later, this mother called me, furious. The nanny had taken the children home from school in a taxi during a rainstorm. "I bring my lunch to work to economize and she's using taxis? She should have taken the bus."

Before I have to rescue another mom from her third-trimester straits, I open up my own brown-bag lunch, with no one to complain to.

I've worked in Washington forever, but when a Mover or a Shaker needs to be rescued I still can't resist her cry for help.

"Mary Matalin called!" my assistant Karen announced several years ago. I was home on a Wednesday, my day off. "Shall I give her your home number or do you want to call her back?"

Matalin had been a political strategist for George Bush Senior and was then in Vice President Cheney's Inner Circle.

I guard my personal numbers with my life, so I asked for Matalin's number. Of course an administration insider like her could have had the Secret Service track me down, but I like the illusion of privacy.

"James and I are expecting our first child," Mary announced, all business. "We'll need a nanny right away."

If you happened to miss it, the bipartisan romance of the nineties began while Matalin was running the Republican presidential campaign and her Democratic counterpart, James Carville, was masterminding Bill Clinton's election. The two politicos fell in love, married, then wrote a book together, *All's Fair: Love, War and Running for President.*

Could I find a nanny resilient enough for the Matalin-Carvilles? "We're not looking for a 'fancy-dancey-nose-in-the-air' type," Mary said. I thought of a few candidates for her until she added, "We'd love the same kind of nanny James had when he was growing up."

She didn't need to say any more. If they grew up north of the Mason-Dixon line, they expect Mary Poppins or Alice from *The Brady Bunch.* If they're from the Deep South, they want me to find them Scarlett O'Hara's mammy. Carville, the Ragin 'Cajun with Attitude, spent his childhood in Louisiana.

Did my client hear me groan? *Gee, Mary*—I tried out the words silently—*we're fresh out of mammies this week.* "I'll do my best," I said cheerily, trying to convey utter confidence. I drove to the office and rummaged through my files to no avail, then called everyone who might lead me to a woman straight out of the antebellum Confederacy. I did have a nanny from Alabama, but she was more Southern belle than Mammy. I'd have to give Mary the bad news and cajole her and James into trying another model.

Then, as if the prayers I should have said were heard anyway, in walked Ella. She'd had years of experience soothing children and their parents, and her former employers said she was "a gift," ageless, warm, and bossy. Ella sounded like she could even stare down Carville, if it came to that. They didn't know it yet, but Mary and James had met their match.

And, sure enough, a priceless relationship was forged over time. Ella rocked both of Mary and James's daughters against her bosom, and watched over them through their toddler years. If Nanny was nearby—as she always was—then all was well. But by the time the girls were in school, Ella was starting to slow down. The family had moved into a larger house, where she tried to chase "her" girls up and down the stairs while holding on to the railing. The job was now too difficult for her.

But Ella's laugh lines had deepened over the years, and there was such trust between them that Mary couldn't seem to initiate the necessary conversation. The woman who handled the press corps with her rapid-fire repartee couldn't tell her nanny that they all had to move on.

Six years after her initial call to White House Nannies, I thought Mary was calling to ask me how on earth she could gracefully let her nanny go. Yes, I was being asked to script one of the best scripters in the business. Mary told the President what to say—and I was supposed to tell her? But I knew the rule: If you're going to fire people—especially people you *love*—let them down easily . . . and take the blame yourself.

"Mary, Ella was the perfect *baby* nanny, but the girls aren't babies anymore. Say you'd never forgive yourself if anything happened to her. You can do this," I said. "You've just got to let her go. Ella will understand."

"Let her go? Barbara, we could never live without Ella! No, I'm just trying to figure out how I'm going to convince her to take a few weeks off. And, when she's back on the job, let me bring in someone to help her. By the way, can you help me find some backup for Ella?"

And that's where the tale would have ended, at "sad, but to be expected," had I not heard the even sadder conclusion. Two weeks later, during her time off, Ella died. She hadn't said a word about being seriously ill to protect her second family from the painful truth.

Moments like these are both highs and lows of my profession. When a nanny joins a family, the results can be funny, remarkable, touching, and tender. Everyone is transformed, including me. Every time I bring parents, children, and caregivers together, I wait to see what will happen because I truly never know.

Nannies keep the District functioning. As the most *present* players inside our Georgetown, Bethesda, and Alexandria homes, many have far more responsibility than "simply" taking care of the children. I'd describe most of the positions I fill, in fact, as Family Management. Nannies do everything the parents don't have time for: train their puppies, get their cars serviced, buy their bosses' bras. One of my clients asked her nanny to fix the dishwasher on Christmas Day. Another nanny booked the family's whitewater-rafting vacation and purchased all the wetsuits.

Thanks for the helpful information," I e-mail Janette after reading her document. Like a lot of other über-parents, Janette and David are determined to do everything perfectly for their child, as if that were possible. (Everything, that is, except being with their children when they're awake.) I need to find a self-confident nanny who won't let these power parents intimidate her; someone smart enough to know which of their demands are reasonable and which to ignore.

But I have no time to find her now, because the phone rings with another emergency. Laura and Charles McKenzie called a few weeks ago to say they were waiting to adopt a baby girl from Korea. This wasn't supposed to happen for several months. But when I hear their breathless excitement all the way from Seoul, I know they got The Call and flew twenty-five hours to pick up their brand-new baby daughter.

Laura had requested a Korean nanny, but she understood that that would be difficult, especially without knowing when her long-dreamed-of child would materialize. At least she and her husband haven't rewritten my application form. The only small challenge to finding the McKenzies a nanny is that their adopted six-month-old daughter has a one-and-a-half-year-old sister who's coming with her. Not every nanny is prepared to handle double duty, so I need to find a strong multitasker who can make cereal with one hand and do a puzzle *and* diaper an infant with the other.

These are only two of my latest requests among the ten families I'm currently juggling. But the truth is, every brand-new Washington baby lands into some kind of already-spring-loaded life. This is matchmaking at its most perilous. So many things can go wrong in the search for a harmonious nanny-family combination in which parents, baby, and nanny all thrive from the initial romance to the sad farewell.

Each new episode sends me back twenty years to my own rude awakening about the true nature of motherhood. I owned the Ice Cream Lobby on Capitol Hill, an oasis where over-worked, underpaid staffers escaped for their frozen fixes.

My sundae menu included the Nancy Reagan: strawberry ice cream and cherry sauce (Nancy liked red) with "fluffy feminine whipped cream surrounded by an adoring circle of California nuts." The Tricky Dick Nixon had two scoops of Rocky Road whitewashed with marshmallow topping: "But someone stole the spoon, so bring your own."

It was exciting to serve, and eavesdrop on, all those political celebrities. Ralph Nader's visit was memorable: I *thought* I gave him the right change for his forty-nine-cent peach ice cream cone until his staffer returned to let me know I'd shortchanged Ralph to the tune of a nickel. (*Plus ça change, plus c'est la même chose?*)

I had the legislators eating out of my hands. "It's the only lobby in town that melts when things get hot," said a Republican rep from Iowa. All those tough congressional decisions, and then they had to choose between praline and banana fudge.

But as much fun as it was to flirt with all those young, cute Hill employees, the babies were even more exciting; I bonded with every one of them, and even the crankiest infant made me dream about my own. And after Richard and I had been married less than a year, Matthew was on his way.

I planned to work until our baby arrived, but pregnancy im-mediately laid me low, and I had to hire someone to take my place. (Why do they call it morning sickness if it strikes around the clock for weeks and months on end, relentlessly?) "Plain cone or sugar?" I asked my customers before I ran into the back room to gag, then returned to finish scooping.

I always knew I'd have a family, but I had no clue what we

were in for when Matt was born. The wonderful baby nurse my in-laws sent me for the first month saved my baby's life as well as mine. Mrs. Boyce was the ultimate professional, a genius at calming Matt down so I could recuperate from his cesarean birth. When she left me for another brand-new mother, I felt like I was losing my best friend. I couldn't stop crying when we hugged good-bye. "Don't be sad that I'm leaving, Mrs. Kline. You'll have plenty else to cry about from now on."

My postpartum depression began the day she left.

Matt was colicky, which pediatricians define as *crying incessantly for reasons no one understands.* He also suffered from gas and constant ear infections. Every time I called the doctor I got the inevitable *Can you hold, please?* By the time a pediatrician was on the line, I was sobbing louder than my baby.

I had *no* experience for this job, not even babysitting; I'd never changed a diaper. I ordered the cloth ones but didn't know I was supposed to wash them before I sent them back. No matter how hard I tried, I couldn't operate a Snugli.

I remembered wanting this baby. But maybe my baby infatuation could only last as long as it took one of them to eat a kiddie-size wafer cone.

Richard called every afternoon, used to hearing me list the dozens of things I'd accomplished in my former life. "What have you been doing?" he asked me sweetly.

"I'm still in my nightgown," I snarled at him. "I haven't eaten, taken a shower, or gotten Matt to stop crying—and you want to know what I've been doing?"

We didn't eat a meal together for months. This is going to sound politically incorrect, and I would never have breathed this to anyone twenty years ago: *I love both my children to pieces. But I never liked taking care of them all day long.*

Maybe my misery was only the temporary, postpartum kind. Or maybe full-time motherhood, filled with tedious, repetitious tasks and unlimited overtime, just wasn't my destiny.

Meanwhile, my student ice-cream crew from Catholic University was carrying gallons of Rocky Road back to the dorms for late-night parties and my profits were melting fast. When Richard realized that my mental health was seriously disintegrating, he practically ordered me back to work. Making banana splits for members of Congress and mopping the floor felt like a vacation in Hawaii compared to being home all day with my son.

So thank goodness I lived in a part of the country, and the world, where there were other mothers who (for one reason or another) couldn't quit their day jobs. "I have a roving mind. If it's not roving in some directed way, it's going to rove somewhere else. I can't just stay in the house," Mary Matalin said in an interview for *Salon*'s "Mothers Who Think" column. But during my early child-rearing years, women didn't say this sort of thing out loud.

"How did you do this?" I moaned to my mother, who was safely far away in northeastern Pennsylvania, with no grandmotherly desire to move near me and pitch in.

"I got help," she said, as if I'd asked a very stupid question. My mother-in-law promised to lend us Mildred, her beloved housekeeper, to take care of Matt. Richard and I could finally go on our long-overdue honeymoon to Lisbon and the Algarve. But shortly before our departure, while I was in my store late at night, putting away the butterscotch topping, I saw someone coming through the glass door. I knew he was trouble before I saw his gun.

Capitol Hill was no safe haven, even though world leaders worked and lived close by. "You're selling the store and we're going to Portugal," my husband announced. *"You're out of there."*

4.

BIRTH OF
A SITCOM

OUR TEN PRECIOUS DAYS in Portugal were great, even though I got food poisoning, which felt like a lethal combination of morning sickness *and* contractions. I spent three days in a fancy tiled *parador* bathroom. We missed our precious Matthew, but not the sleepless nights or the constant stream of temporary babysitters.

Which both resumed as soon as we got home and had to send Mildred back to my mother-in-law in Florida. Now that I'd sold the shop and Matthew was my world, my playmate, and my boss, I was in serious shock. Reading Dr. Seuss out loud incessantly was making me lose IQ points. And I'm not the playground type.

By now Matt was crawling at top speed, with a vengeance. He was so unpredictable and active, I couldn't take my eyes off him. When Matt was six months old, we hired a young Bolivian woman named Marta who sounded as energetic as our son. "Her references are *great,*" I was told, so frantic I never even called them.

But this time I was lucky. Marta could actually keep up with our whirling-dervish boy; she was happy to get down on the floor with him, take him to the park, and push him on the swing for hours. Her English was shaky, and she wasn't yet a legal U.S. resident. But in 1983, ten years before the Nannygate scandal, this was still a small detail. Richard and I agreed to fill out pages of forms to sponsor Marta so she'd eventually be working legally.

Now that we had such enthusiastic, reliable help, I didn't have to be a genius to figure out my next career. I'd spent months along with all my friends searching for reliable childcare, when our babies let us. The agencies I called did all the talking and none of the listening; as a result, they sent me all the wrong people.

I'd always had a good rapport with the young women who worked in my ice-cream shop, so I knew I'd enjoy talking to potential nannies. After a few days in the library and a lot of phone calls, I discovered a woman in the Midwest who knew how to find experienced girls who'd be thrilled to work for Washington families.

My old Goucher College roommate, Martha Connolly, who had become a psychiatric social worker, gave me important screening advice. I wanted to make sure my potential nannies were emotionally whole and mature enough to care for young children. "Find out about their childhoods," she said, "and if they have a good relationship with their mothers."

As the business section of the *Washington Post* reported in 1996, White House Nannies originally sounded more like a sitcom than a terrific business idea. My father-in-law offered me free office space for what he considered my new hobby. I finally had a serious mission, and a reason to get out of my faded sweat ensembles. "At least your business will get you out of the house and away from the stores," my husband said.

My best friend, Shelley, a divorce attorney (big business in D.C.) who needed to get back to work, was my first client. I sent her Alicia. Back in Montana, she'd helped raise her seven brothers and sisters, and she knew more about taking care of children than Shelley and I put together. She had big '80s hair, and she wore white pumps in the middle of winter and too much Poison by Christian Dior, but Alicia's common sense and always-can-do attitude won our hearts. White House Nannies took off immediately. My phone number made its way around suburban playgrounds and dinner parties so fast I didn't even have to advertise.

And most important, I was connected to others, to the "outside" world again. I was meeting a special breed of women and introducing them to fascinating families. I'd read about my clients in the paper, seen them on television, and discussed their policies and personalities at dinner parties.

Now I was inside their homes, witnessing very different kinds of Washington stories: real *unspun* ones.

Finally, my life was in balance. Families with new babies were just as cheerful customers as the staffers who ordered ice-cream cones. But now I had a white-collar job. And at the end of the day, I was thrilled to get home to my family.

Meanwhile, our amazingly industrious Marta fit right into our family. She worked hard on her English, then went to night school and got her GED. Alone in this country with no one to depend on, Marta moved herself forward with determination, always taking us by surprise with her latest success. In fact, she learned to "work the system" so efficiently, she decided to take off minor holidays, the ones only federal employees get around here. Richard and I had to work on those days, of course.

"Gee, Marta," I remember asking her one October 12. "Did Columbus discover *Bolivia,* too?"

Soon the joke around our house was that *we* were working for *Marta,* but we admired her pluck. By the time I was pregnant with my daughter, Gillian, we needed a full-fledged live-in nanny, but Marta was too busy with her college classes, so we both had to move on.

Even though I was in the nanny business, it wasn't easy finding my own close-to-perfect one. Every great candidate had several families to choose from. But eventually Wendy from Minnesota became my children's new best friend, and she stayed with us for a year and a half. It was a good thing I now had a daughter, because Wendy *adored* little girls. (Ever since Wendy, I ask nannies if they have a preference for girls or boys.)

Next came Kayla, a wholesome-sounding Mormon who didn't smoke or drink caffeine or liquor. But our syrupy-sweet nanny had come to D.C. on a religious mission to find Mr. Right, and she met a different prospect every night of the week at her youth group.

Kayla took *pretty* good care of Matt and Gillian—not counting the time my daughter almost fell down the cellar stairs while Kayla was giving herself a facial. If I hadn't dropped in for a surprise visit, which I suggest all parents do, I'd have found out too late, in the emergency room, that our nanny wasn't devoted to her job.

On her very last day with us, Kayla asked if she could borrow our car to go to church. How could we refuse? My mother had given us her thirteen-year-old Mercedes so our nanny would be able to transport the children. It was perfectly maintained, but it leaked oil; Kayla knew she had to check the gauge *every* time she drove it.

When she finally called at dinnertime, we were frantic; Kayla must have been too blinded by the Lord's light to notice the light on the oil gauge, so my mother's vintage Mercedes engine had seized up and died.

I can't say I tapped into a gold mine, but White House Nannies catapulted me into what felt like the District limelight. One of my very first clients was a secretary of defense and his wife, an intimidating couple to say the least, especially Mrs. Secretary. In those days, I always made a house visit to get to know the parents and see where the nanny would live. This McLean, Virginia, home was on such an exclusive street I could barely find it, a hidden enclave full of government big shots where I soon had many other clients.

The young woman I found for this couple was a bit naive. Okay, I admit it—she wasn't very bright. I still ask myself why I put *her* with those particularly intense parents. For one thing, she ended up breaking many of the treasures they'd collected during their postings abroad. "When can I start charging her?" the mother called to ask.

The not-very-smart nanny met my nanny, Wendy, also from Minnesota. After Wendy took her to the beach at Ocean City, Maryland, she reported back to me that the nanny had actually asked her which ocean they were swimming in.

But even more alarming was the fact that this nanny seemed to constantly lose her house keys. She finally made copies and passed out the keys to all her friends, so she'd never be locked out again. If the secretary of defense had found out how defenseless he was with his house keys all over town, I could have had a very short career.

Finding a nanny for parents anywhere is a tricky proposition. You're playing God by creating brand-new families. Most professional mothers in this town are in such hot pursuit of their particular kind of success that they need lots and lots of childcare, usually from Day One. There's such a shortage of domestic help in our country that for the last several decades, foreigners have filled the gap.

Many of these women from other countries used to provide this childcare illegally, and their employers avoided paying unemployment and health insurance for them. But that was before Zoe Baird's illegal Peruvian help prevented her from becoming our first female Attorney General. Ever since Nannygate, *we're legal here.*

Ms. Baird assumed responsibility for her lapse in judgment, and she blamed it on the "pressures of motherhood." This working mother's plight touched a national nerve. Thousands of constituents called their senators either in sympathy with Zoe Baird or to complain about the high-earning, high-profile, tax-dodging couple.

"There is a dirty little secret in middle- and upper-middle-class America," The *Wall Street Journal* reported about the scandal. "Nannies are among the most exploited workers in the country." Kimba Wood, another Attorney General nominee, and Linda Chavez, Secretary of Labor designate, both had to withdraw their nominations for the same tax and employment law violations.

In the past, women were always in the headlines for these nanny transgressions. Congratulations, Bernie Kerik! He was going to be our head of Homeland Security, in charge of all immigration issues. Bernie, *what were you thinking?* Maybe his illegal nanny didn't seem like a problem in New York, but any professionally ambitious Washington parent knows enough by now to play strictly by the rules. They make sure to hire either domestic or documented foreign help, and pay their social security, disability, and unemployment "nanny" taxes.

Not every agency plays by these rules, by the way, even today. Listen hard for code words: *Her papers are in progress . . . there are just a few details to sort out . . . we assume you won't mind sponsoring her?* But if you're even remotely involved with government, the military, non-profits, law, industry, or the media, your entire existence might be mercilessly scrutinized at any moment. Since everyone in D.C. thinks they'll be the next federal trade commissioner, Cabinet member, or Supreme Court justice, all parents here have to be beyond reproach. That's why I refer clients to Stephanie Breedlove, my domestic tax guru in Austin, Texas.

These days, there are even more restrictions and hoops to jump through to help someone move through the legal process. I was asked to participate in a Senate commission on immigration reform during that watershed year of 1993 to discuss the childcare crisis. Along with twenty other "experts," I sat at a horseshoe-shaped table while Senator Edward Kennedy and Cardinal Bernard Law heard us all testify that there weren't enough legally authorized, skilled providers to meet the enormous and still-growing demand for childcare and home-care workers.

The situation hasn't changed. Experienced childcare workers, experts at *the most important job there is,* are still considered "unskilled labor" in this country, even though they're respected professionals in other countries. Lady Diana Spencer was among those certified for the job in Great Britain. But highly qualified individuals aren't allowed to fill these vital jobs here until they're granted legal status.

I informed the esteemed Senate commission that my agency

had to turn away the majority of our job applicants because they weren't legal residents. The committee's conclusions were surprising news: There aren't enough legal childcare providers in our country, and we have a crisis on our hands. And that was that. Today, more than ten years later, there are still no real solutions in the pipeline.

An Ivy League economist at the hearing that day actually suggested we resolve our childcare issues by employing former prisoners in these positions to help integrate them back into society. So far, *that* hasn't happened. But it goes without saying that the dearth of competent people for both private and public childcare positions is even worse today, everywhere in the country.

Laura and Charles McKenzie, for instance, will arrive at Dulles International in three days with their new daughters. Charles has already used up his paternity leave from a Rockville biotech company on the time-consuming Korean double adoption, and Laura has to be back at the Pentagon, in her words, "as soon as possible if not sooner." Her entire department is thrilled about her sudden fortune, but Laura will have to fit her two new projects into an already-crammed agenda.

As soon as the McKenzies alerted me, I asked Lilly from the Philippines if she was still free. "The McKenzie job has changed a bit," I said, mentioning the augmented salary. Lilly once worked for a family with twins, so she's well prepared for the Korean sisters. She'll think about it. But in case she turns it down, I need to find a backup.

Time to call my friendly competitor, Nancy Gillis, who runs her own placement agency called Nanny Nation. We warn each other about "difficult" parents on the prowl; some of them hire us both simultaneously. We also alert each other about any bad apples in the nanny barrel.

"Got anyone for two little Korean girls?" I ask her, certainly not expecting a yes. "It would be great if the woman knows a few words in their native tongue." It's always fun to make Nancy laugh, even at my expense.

"I did talk to a young Japanese woman," she thinks out loud. "But she's way too delicate to handle two children." Nannies willing to start *now* are in short supply this week, but what else is new?

"Thanks anyway," I say. "I'll just resort to prayer at this point."

By the time I'm ready to go home and start my *other* job— gourmet chef for my husband and teenagers—Lilly, the nanny I *knew* was right for the McKenzies, calls to say she'll accept the position. She's even agreed to meet Laura and Charles at the airport and help them settle in. That's what I call going beyond the call of duty, always a thrilling act of human kindness to witness.

5.

SEARCHING FOR
KARMA

AFTER A WONDERFUL MEAL, I unwind in the den with a glass of wine to watch a radiant, about-to-deliver Janette Huntington reporting from the North Lawn. I never look that good, no matter how much money I spend on my hair, and I'm not eight months pregnant. According to the *Post*'s "Reliable Source" column, Lorraine Aprile does Janette's hair, along with the rest of the network crowd. I wonder if I can get an appointment.

"The President highlights the accomplishments of his administration's first year," Janette reports. Security, tax relief, an education bill, environmental cleanup, and a new energy plan. This must be her last broadcast because her due date looms on the horizon. I'm surprised she isn't doing a special report about Washington's childcare crisis. She's as calm and collected as usual, so you'd never know she's dealing with her own disaster. And I'm the designated superheroine. No problem, I tell myself. I'm used to saving my clients' careers.

Mental note for Monday: *Janette. Front burner.*

Because I was fortunate enough to work for myself while my kids were young, I didn't have to make the excruciatingly difficult choices that my clients like Janette face. These striving District mothers endure endless office hours, constant travel, and random requests for professional face time no matter when.

They don't have the privilege of watching their kids' school plays, making snacks for the lacrosse team, or even staying home when a child is sick. Or when they are. They have to run whatever 90-hour-a-week show they're in *and* find high-quality time for their kids. The word "juggle" doesn't quite capture it.

But every working mother who hands her children over to someone else places her very soul in a stranger's care. No amount of money is enough to pay for this peace of mind. As one nanny-dependent woman once said, "If I had a million dollars, I'd give half to my nanny." I wish more of my clients felt that way.

I skim through all thirty questions on each nanny's application we receive, looking for clues about each candidate. We get our share of college grads with no idea what to do with their literature, sociology, and women's studies degrees. I had no idea what to do with mine, either.

A college education is not a prerequisite for this job, but if the woman claims to have gone to college, it had better be true. One woman's résumé stated she graduated from George Washington

University, so I was surprised when her potential employer, an attorney at Akin, Gump and a G.W.U. trustee, checked and found out that his potential nanny was, instead, a George Washington dropout.

Too bad. It wouldn't have mattered if she'd never attended a college class. And now the point was: She lied.

Thanks to that savvy client, now I do education checks, too.

We used to ask about an applicant's height, weight, and emotional and physical health until an irate (overweight) nanny's employer, who happened to be an EEOC attorney, took up her cause. Now I know the Americans with Disabilities Act by heart. However, there are code words to watch out for. If a nanny's hobbies are crocheting, knitting, doing cross-stitch, baking, or *watching* sports on television, I assume she's the sedentary type. I want to go on record here: A nanny can be heavy but also able to run around after active children and be *stellar* in her job.

I'm also on the lookout for women who want a job for the wrong reasons. "Baby bonders" yearn to be mothers themselves and are thrilled to practice on someone else's children before they have their own. They're only in the game for the short haul. Barbara Bush's chief of staff, Susan Porter Rose, interviewed a young, extremely well-spoken woman from the West who we thought was a winner. Until she asked how often she'd be coming to the White House, and if she could work there part-time while Ms. Rose's son was in school.

I have to give nannies the bad news: They're not being hired for their employer's job.

After we found Susan another nanny, I got to have lunch at the Executive Mess. There's no greater thrill, even for a longtime Washingtonian, than being invited to 1600 Pennsylvania Avenue.

This kind of matchmaking is always complex. The nanny one set of parents adores might wreak havoc in a different home. These potential saints and saviors come from near and far, and they're as amazingly varied as the families who hire them. In addition to Spanish, French, and Mandarin, our nannies speak Singhalese, Urdu, Tagalog, and Wollof. Some were raised by nannies themselves, and some take care of Washington children to support their own, who live very far away.

Because I bring together nannies and families from such different backgrounds, cross-cultural surprises are bound to occur. One mother, whose baby was teething, noticed her Haitian nanny's unusual home remedies. She held the child up to the sun whenever possible and rubbed his head with alcohol. The mother found the nanny praying over the child in a dark, candlelit basement room. Even though the nanny's bizarre techniques seemed to calm the teething baby down, she was fired. So much for cultural tolerance.

Sometimes these backgrounds clash. An energetic, experienced Wisconsin farm girl just never felt *comfortable* with the Georgetown society family she worked for. The parents dragged the children to cocktail parties and pricey restaurants and expected the nanny to keep them under control.

"I can't believe she's unhappy," the socialite complained. When I explained that the young woman was out of her comfort zone lunching at the Four Seasons, the mother was flabbergasted. "That lunch wasn't fancy at all," she insisted. "The children only had grilled-cheese sandwiches." Did I need to tell her it wasn't about what the children ordered?

I found this wonderful nanny another job with a down-to-earth, *actually working* mom whose idea of a special lunch was sandwiches at the Parkway Deli.

When it comes to unpredictable matches, I was a bit concerned that the daughter of a Mormon bishop wouldn't feel totally at home with a rabbi and his family. But this interfaith great marriage was a success. The nanny learned how to keep kosher and prepare a Passover dinner, and the children got to visit the awe-inspiring Mormon temple that rises out of the Beltway like the Magic Kingdom.

Good nannies are so valuable in Washington, they get to choose their positions. How many children are there and how old are they? What about the neighborhood a nanny will live in? I've heard nannies deliberate between a swimming pool and a new Lexus, between a month of paid vacation and a trip to Europe with the family. Stock options and signing bonuses are also common nanny lures.

I've heard it said that nannies actually *run* this town, and even though this might be a bit of an exaggeration, the families I work with would fall apart without them. And then what would happen to our government?

Who should I send to Janette and David? I refax them *my* Employer's Application for Childcare, hoping it will buy me a little time. But the application shoots back at me within an hour, meticulously filled in. Janette and her husband are willing to pay whatever they have to for a dedicated, totally reliable nanny.

There aren't many choices in my Currently Available folder. Janette needs a self-starter, a great communicator, and an excellent driver who can navigate D.C.'s congested maze. She'll have to run the Huntington-Wilder household smoothly—without much input from her employers.

David has clients all over the world, and Janette has to cover the President no matter where he is. Nanny will have to cope resourcefully with earaches and other emergencies—if she can't prevent them from occurring in the first place. *Most* important, she'll have to adore Janette and David's firstborn and his or her future siblings. Like most of the families I work with, she's going to spend a lot more time with the baby than his parents will.

If only I could find them another Cheryl, the nanny who helped Larry Summers and his attorney wife, Victoria, raise three children and run their household. That fourteen-year nanny-family partnership was worthy of a congressional medal. From the very beginning, the Summers wanted her to share their Washington experience as well as their childcare. The whole family, including Cheryl, stood together in the Oval Office while Summers was sworn in as Secretary of the Treasury. The nanny also attended the annual Renaissance Democratic get-together at Hilton Head, where her boss insisted on introducing her to President Clinton, assuring him that Cheryl's job was as important to him as the President's. And she enjoyed another kind of Washington experience when Bono came to town, and her employer invited Cheryl for dinner with him at Galileo.

Like many of our nannies who work for divorced families, Cheryl remained close with both employers after their divorce. When Summers became president of Harvard, she helped set up his new home in Cambridge. Clients of mine who know her always ask me for a nanny just like Cheryl.

I'm imagining an All-American type. The loyal, devoted Midwestern girls are no longer as common as they were when I first started this business, but they're still around. In the '80s, they sent in glamour shots along with their résumés, as if they were applying for modeling jobs. In those days their primary goal was simply getting out of Idaho or Montana or Wyoming. And there was culture shock when they realized that my clients wanted their children to eat exotic foods like fresh fish and cauliflower.

But Janette needs a variation on this theme: an industrious self-starter who'll be able to read her employers' minds but be smart enough to know when *not* to read them. Some college classes must appear on her résumé, as she'll be in charge of the baby's formal education as soon as she arrives.

One of the highest-paid nannies I ever placed was a fifty-five-year-old divorcée and former museum docent whose daughter attended Yale. Say no more. A nanny like this could have unleashed a Chevy Chase feeding frenzy: Any child in her care was *guaranteed* an Ivy admission eighteen years down the road as well.

Confession time. I understand this parental desire to hire a nanny who'll bring out the children's inner genius. I was seduced by Allison, a Seven Sisters graduate, when Matt and Gillian were at the Potomac School. When I picked up our potential nanny for a tryout afternoon with my children, I remember Matt shouting, "What's a polygon?" from the backseat on our way home. I'd stopped trying to decipher my kids' math homework as soon as they got to fourth grade.

"It's a shape with three or more straight sides," Allison shot back.

I was hooked.

But superachiever Allison really wanted to be working for a Fortune 500 company instead of doing my kids' laundry. I found our bright, fastidious nanny scrubbing my counters at two A.M., and she brushed her teeth until her gums bled. I was glad my kids were getting A's, but this was my first experience with obsessive-compulsive disorder.

One more thing to watch out for when screening nannies.

Kathleen and Chris Matthews had much better luck with the Mount Holyoke graduate I sent them that same month. Gianna cared for their three children while Kathleen anchored the local news and Chris was making his national mark with *Hardball,* no walk in the park. That turned out to be a nanny-family match made in heaven. Gianna still describes Kathleen as her ultimate role model, the multitasker of all time. "She can get home from work and give a fabulous dinner party an hour later. And she's totally relaxed the entire time!" according to Gianna. "Kathleen and Chris truly love one another and they're so devoted to those children."

And by the way, we just sent a nanny to help Gianna with her *own* newborn child.

But back to Janette, whose time-frame and *slightly* excessive expectations make her application a bit challenging. I've been here a thousand times. But after hours of file-foraging, I come up with two possibilities. Neither sounds amazing, but you can never tell. Often the nanny-family combinations I'm most worried about turn out to be the longest-lasting.

Janette's inevitable call comes through around noon. "Just checking in," she chirps. Purposefully upbeat, as if she's totally *over* Closetgate. But I detect the ton of pressure behind that mellifluous voice. My currently most important client assumes that everything will go smoothly for her family from this moment on. The closet catastrophe means she's paid her dues.

"Just choosing between the best of the best for you," I stall gracefully. I can be chipper under pressure, too.

"What have you got?" She tries not to sound impatient while en route to a press conference. I can read the headlines in her mind: FBI, CIA, and Childcare.

I'm not going to unearth any more decent candidates this

week or maybe even this month, so I give Janette my short—and only—list. "Polly Childs is taking a year off from American University and seems very smart; she babysits all over Spring Valley and has great references, but she's going to be a short-termer. She has too much of a personal life."

"Who else do you have?"

"Donna Ann Halsey was the oldest sibling in her large Minnesota family."

"Do you know I'm from Minnesota?" Janette laughs.

I love it when there's karma. Donna's credentials are better than a poli-sci degree, but Janette doesn't understand that yet. Donna is no fashion plate; frumpy is more like it. But she'll be steadfast, and she can handle the weight of this job.

"I'll have my assistant set up appointments for tomorrow," Janette says.

The next day the verdict's in. "Well, Polly is adorable. But she wants to take massage-therapy classes two nights a week, and I can't promise I'll be home on time. But you were right about Donna. She reminds me of the girls I went to high school with," she says nostalgically. "She was in the Four-H club, too!" Janette starts to tell me about her rabbit-breeding project. The secret lives of public personalities are always interesting.

"Great choice," I tell her. Donna's a sure bet, competent and steady as they come. She's had the same boyfriend forever, a soldier at Fort Mead, and she's available any time. After growing up in a house with five siblings, Donna's thrilled about having her own room and full bath in Janette and David's roomy Colonial.

"It's all good," she assures me on the phone, and I assume this includes the closets. She'll move in before the baby nurse leaves, so Mrs. Plumb can give her the lay of the land.

I have a feeling that'll be an interesting relationship.

We're almost there. When my contract arrives fresh from David's law firm, I'm not surprised he's crossed out the clause protecting White House Nannies from being sued for willful negligence. Have any attorney-clients *ever* simply signed the document and sent it back?

6.

THE REIGN OF
OVERPRICED PLUMB

AMILY AND MEDICAL LEAVE is a matter of pure common
sense and a matter of common decency. It will provide
Americans what they need most: peace of mind. Never
again will parents have to fear losing their jobs because of their
families," President Clinton said after signing his landmark federal
law in 1993. For the first time in our country's history, employees had the right to time off for family or health issues without
fear of being demoted or losing their jobs altogether.

We all thought this would change things, but unfortunately,
many of my clients can't manage to take advantage of this landmark law.

Janette works her normal twelve- to fifteen-hour days until
Week 38. But for the two weeks before her due date, she only
takes assignments close to home and to Sibley Hospital—known
as Hotel Sibley for its well-appointed birthing suites.

Her baby must know that his power parents expect things to happen on schedule, because I read in the *Washington Post* Style section that Spencer Huntington-Wilder was born right on time. Janette's water broke twenty minutes after she taped the President's briefing with Secretary Rumsfeld, and Spencer was born six hours later. I hope Janette and David don't expect him to always be this cooperative.

As soon as Janette's forty-eight hours of managed-care pampering are over, she and David take their wonder child home. Richard Nixon lived in this same Spring Valley neighborhood of leafy trees and wide sidewalks. In his era there was a covenant barring residents from selling their homes to African Americans or Jews.

The freezer is stocked with a month's worth of healthy meals, and the baby nurse has put away all the baby gifts and organized the nursery for action. Even though David has bought cartons of disposables, Mrs. Plumb insists on a diaper service—only cloth nappies would do for *her* babies.

Despite a few hormonal mood swings and a touch of anemia, Janette has sailed through pregnancy and childbirth. She's proud of herself for winning the baby-nurse sweepstakes, and for being lucky enough to pay three hundred and fifty dollars a day for the British-National-Nursery-Board-Certified, take-charge Nurse Plumb. Her friends have assured her it's worth every penny to be in such good hands.

Janette's afraid to give up her on-air face time any longer than necessary. The younger eager beaver filling in for her hopes she'll trade in her microphone for the hobby of motherhood. Her bureau chief calls to congratulate her: "Don't worry about the time off. Lisa's doing a terrific job."

Maybe I can get back sooner, she thinks. *Why take a chance?*

Some mothers I work with do take their entire two- or three-month maternity leaves. By American standards, this is considered luxurious. In Europe, however, even the most career-driven parents take months and even years to have and raise their children.

Occasionally, a D.C. husband takes his paternity leave right after his wife goes back to work, so he can bond with the baby, too.

I lied.

The one dad I know who took advantage of this enlightened family-leave policy committed career suicide.

David's paternity leave was supposed to be two weeks, but at the last minute he was told the firm just couldn't spare him. No surprise there. When a lawyer recently called me in a sweat, I could hear his infant sobbing in the background.

"You must be home on paternity leave," I said.

"I was *supposed* to have some time," he laughed. "But my biggest case heated up right before Ethan was born, so that was that. I missed my window of opportunity. Do you watch *The Sopranos?*" he goes on. "It's all about being an *earner.* And earners don't get leave."

Every attorney, male or female, tells me the same thing. A new-parent lawyer in Foggy Bottom is lucky to spend a four-day weekend with his or her newborn. And they'd better keep their screaming infant far away from the phone when they're on a conference call.

David's four days at home seems like a huge amount of time off, as close to a vacation as he and Janette can remember spending together. Every so often one of them takes a break from bonding with Spencer to peek at a BlackBerry, when the other one isn't looking.

David finally calls me. "Since our nanny is starting in a month, I just wanted to make sure I figured out her withholding tax correctly," he says.

"How are things going?" I ask. I can tell something else is on his mind. The pedigreed baby nurse should have everything under control, so what could be the problem? The poor guy goes straight into confessional mode. "The baby nurse is driving my wife crazy."

"I thought I wanted a take-charge type," Janette whispers when I call her. "I have hardly any time left with Spencer, and I can't get him away from you-know-who. We call her Mrs. Prune! *'Please, Mrs. Huntington-Wilder. Don't go into the nursery. I just put him down.'* She won't let anyone near Spencer. Not even my parents."

I've heard this tale before. The fancier your baby nurse, the harder it can be to remember you're the baby's mother. Cabinet members, ambassadors, and judges who thought they did the right thing have asked me to send their nannies *immediately.* So they can get rid of the pedigreed Knightsbridge drill sergeants my clients *thought* they hired to help them bond with their babies—instead of ordering them around in their own homes and nurseries.

At least Janette does have exclusive breast-feeding privileges. Even if the strictly old-school Mrs. Plumb is *horrified* that a respectable woman would do something so *primitive.* "That's fine for third-world countries, or maybe for those hippies in California," she says, "but babies need dependable, carefully measured formula feedings."

This makes Janette even more determined to nurse Spencer, at least a few times a day, just to spite her reactionary warden. Her hospital-grade, $300 pump will allow her to express and freeze enough antibody-rich nutrition for Spencer after she's back at work.

Despite her tearful, valiant attempts and a few sessions with a compassionate lactation consultant, breast-feeding is too agonizing an ordeal. No matter how hard she tries and how sore it makes her nipples, Janette can't produce enough milk for her ravenous, frantic baby. For the first time in her life, she's not so good at something. The lactation counselor assures her it's just a case of unfortunate physiology, but our correspondent can't forgive herself for her first bad grade at true motherhood.

"Oh, *really?*" a competitive new-mother friend says after Janette makes the mistake of confiding in her. "That's *so* disappointing." Janette can hear the hardly disguised disdain. Soon her abject failure will be all over town. "The *least* I can do is breast-feed my baby," she says, a line I've heard from so many rushing-back-to-work parents.

The new mothers I know are determined to be as successful in the maternity department as they are in the State Department. Many engage in covert maternal activities in the Capitol and Senate ladies' rooms behind doors with Pumping in Progress signs. But this behavior is often considered unprofessional.

One blue-suited client put her bottles of expressed milk in the break-room freezer, which caused some tension in the office. "My immediate [female] supervisor thought I was wasting my precious time and energy trying to be Earth Mother," she told me. "I said it was a medical necessity because if I don't pump, I'll get mastitis. The men I work for are far more understanding than the women."

Today's pumping professional camouflages her state-of-the-art equipment in a special briefcase to maintain her businesslike image. One client had me in hysterics when she told me how she ruined that image the morning her breast pump got stuck in the door of her commuter train.

Mrs. Plumb can hardly hide her satisfaction when Janette, feeling like a total failure, finally abandons her breast-feeding plan. "Now I get it," she tells me. "The less my baby needs me, the more he needs the Prune."

Mrs. Plumb will have the baby all to herself soon enough, as Janette is taking the shortest maternity leave she can manage. Network dynamos like Judy Woodruff and Leslie Stahl didn't enjoy months of baby-bonding time at home, either, and Janette is afraid one of the new kids on the block will steal her visibility.

She'll miss those tender moments with her child. But at least she'll get away from Plumb.

Janette is ready to pick up where she left off at the network. Those thousand-dollar suits fit her perfectly again, thanks to her trainer. In fact, if she hadn't built the exercise room downstairs, the nanny suite would have bigger closets.

As soon as she reports back to duty, she has to dash to the Hill for an Armed Services Committee hearing. Even though her baby nurse made sure she got enough sleep, she's been studying newborn development instead of the defense budget, so she'll have to fake it.

There were tears in her eyes when she kissed her baby's sleeping head and marched out the door, but they're gone by the time she reports for duty. If half of D.C. hadn't received the Tiffany announcement, no one would know her life is any different.

Efficient Mrs. Plumb has maneuvered Spencer into routine naps and feedings, and the only night he doesn't sleep eight hours is Plumb's night off, just to prove his parents are inept at their latest and most important occupation. Donna from Minnesota will be a breath of fresh Midwestern air—someone Janette can relate to, and who won't make her feel like an intruder in her own home.

Before she leaves for New York to take charge of a new set of unsuspecting parents, Overpriced Plumb has agreed to spend a few days teaching Donna what she needs to know about her new charge and his parents. In this town, new parents are far too busy, and sometimes too clueless, to train their nannies, so they prefer to pay for what's known as "the overlap," to save them time and energy.

But the overlap can backfire. When Donna calls me in a rage, I'm the first to find out that this isn't a smooth transition. "She won't let me *near* the baby," she wails. "She checks his bathwater and his formula with a *thermometer!*"

"She's out of there in another day," I tell her. "And you're going to love this job."

Fortunately, Janette and David are safely far away at work, so they never know about the war in their own home.

After I put out that brushfire, my assistant Karen runs in. "When you have an hour to spare, Barbara, please call Elise!" She laughs—another in-house joke.

I'm *spent,* but I figure I can listen to Elise while I read applications or declutter my desk. She's a clinical psychologist known for helping congressmen's wives adjust to inside-the-Beltway abandonment. I used to call her Dr. Shipler, but now we've bonded. Elise Shipler is funny and charming, and I actually like her; if I needed—and had time for—some counseling myself, I'd even go to her.

Or maybe we should do a trade, because now that I've sent Elise a nanny she adores, she assumes, like many of my clients, that my fee covers unlimited post-placement phone-therapy sessions.

"I know you're busy," she says breathlessly. Elise lives in Adams Morgan, not the most exclusive neighborhood, and when she got home yesterday, her nanny had forgotten to lock the door.

"Maybe I hired the wrong person," she says, completely frazzled. "I'm starting to question my own judgment!"

I tell Elise to tell her nanny to be more vigilant; there have been break-ins on her street. I also give her the name of a handyman who can change her locks and install an alarm system. Dr. Shipler thinks I'm brilliant.

"I knew you were the perfect person to help me process this," she says. I've never found the nerve to ask her, or any client who calls me for technical or emotional troubleshooting, if I can charge for it—at the going rate. Maybe I'll ask my lawyer if we can write it into the contract.

But at least Elise Shipler observes the fifty-minute rule.

I'm looking forward to a leftover-salad lunch, at my desk. My daughter, Gillian, forgot to take her tennis racket to school this morning—again—so I have to drive home and get it, then drive from Bethesda to Potomac in time for her four o'clock match—in an hour. (*Please, Mom. The coach is going to kill me!*)

Forget about eating that salad.

Then the phone rings.

I'm always eager to talk to a new client. This time it's a dad. Jeffrey Darwin can hardly wait to tell me all about his thirteen-thousand-square-foot starter castle, his Olympic pool, his wine cellar, and the basketball celebrity who used to own the place. Nothing, by the way, about his children. Is he just calling to discuss real estate?

Fathers are usually less descriptive than their wives about the kind of nanny they're looking for. But even though Jeffrey Darwin is full of details, none of his information is helpful. When I finally interrupt his bragging and find out his current nanny is eighteen years old and from Utah, I hear a warning bell. A woman that young is usually in D.C. on a kind of "junior year abroad," so thrilled to get out of the Midwest that she'll work for slave wages.

My new client obviously had the cash to choose a less risky model. But Jeffrey Darwin hired inexperienced Mormon labor because he's cheap.

"We love Jenna," Jeffrey tells me. "But she's going back to school full-time, so we need another Jenna as soon as possible."

When a nanny leaves a job under less-than-wonderful circumstances, *I'm going back to college* is a convenient excuse. But I don't pry at the moment.

"We're having a new baby in a month, and our twin boys are starting third grade at Landon." Not a private school for parents on a budget. Next I hear that Jeffrey drives a 3200 GT Maserati convertible and his wife tools around in their Lexus SUV.

"Do you have a car for the nanny?"

"Oh, yeah. The '88 Taurus." I'm not sure why I need to know so much about the Darwin automotive fleet. But I do know they'd rather invest in property and toys than pay their nanny a living wage.

It's Friday afternoon, I've been charming for five days straight, and I'm talking to a guy with plenty of disposable income who's a cheapskate when it comes to the most important expense he has. I know where this is going, so I let my feelings fly.

"So it's important to send your children to Landon, but you're looking to economize on the third-most-vital person in their lives?" There's an edge to my voice because I'm aggravated enough not to care. "I don't think we can work together." I'm practically shouting at the guy and I could not care less.

Maserati Man turns into a puppy. Why is it that as soon as I tell someone they don't qualify for my services, they do a one-eighty and practically beg me to take them on—at any price? As you may have guessed, the nanny who moves into the Darwin Potomac palace ends up with $15 an hour instead of the $8 Jeffrey was paying his last nanny.

Meanwhile, things must be calm again in Spring Valley *chez* Janette and David. The first few weeks of any nanny's employ are full of surprises, but it's the adjustment period. Food issues are the most common. Janette and David are shocked that Donna isn't familiar with their South Beach diet and would rather stick to her carb-loaded meals: potatoes, creamed corn, and *white bread,* which Janette hasn't seen since she grew up on Minnesota hotdish casserole.

When I asked a prospective nanny I wanted to send to a highly sophisticated family if she cooked, she asked if I meant a *whole* meal! (Which part of the meal was she thinking of eliminating?) Midwestern meat-and-potato nannies often still have problems with the concepts of fresh vegetables and fish. My neighbor was horrified when Nanny fed the children hot dog-pineapple-marshmallow kabobs. "When I suggested something green, she made the kids lime Jell-O," she told me.

But some nannies know more about nutrition than their employers. A pediatrician gave his son super-sweet breakfast cereal every morning; then the nanny had to deal with the hyped-up child all day. When she told the father his son was going nuts from the sugar, he informed her there were no proven studies connecting Cap'n Crunch to hyperactivity.

Donna is at least familiar with canned vegetables, but when

Janette asks her to run to Sutton Gourmet and pick up tuna for dinner, Donna brings back three cans of Chicken of the Sea.

"She's great with the baby, and a lovely person," Janette reports. I brace myself for whatever the problem is. "I know this sounds *petty*. But Donna's clothes are *pathetic*."

I hear it all the time: "The nanny should look good when she picks my child up at school. After all, *she represents us*."

One of my mothers who works in corporate finance, the navy-suit-and-low-pumps type, opened her door, ready to interview a candidate I'd highly recommended. "Her breasts were absolutely *horizontal*," the flustered mother told me. "She looked like a *call girl*! All of a sudden, my husband and my fifteen-year-old son were only too anxious to help me interview this nanny."

Whoops—I guess I should have coached that nanny about dressing for success.

D o you think it's okay if I give Donna a gift certificate to the Gap?" Janette asks me. "Kind of like a clothing allowance?" Spencer's Petit Bateau onesies are imported from France, and a personal shopper puts together *her* wardrobe, so maybe she feels a little guilty about her nanny's Salvation Army collection.

"That's a great idea," I say.

J anette is back in intense action, working her normal sixty-plus hours a week, not counting emergencies. She's sure she can produce the way she always did, if not better. Her first week on the air I see her boarding Air Force One to Denver, a PR trip for President Bush's new policy on the environment. She's standing in the middle of the Rockies with the Colorado wind blowing through her hair. She's glowing as if she doesn't have a care in the world and her nanny problems are over.

And I certainly hope they are. Donna's settled into her new job and has started to eat fresh vegetables. She looks great in her khakis and white shirts from The Gap, and things seem to be going quite well. Spencer's a happy baby, even though he doesn't see a lot of his parents, Donna says. I've made another successful marriage, and there's no better feeling.

I put Janette's case in my Seems to Be Going Well file. I'm not naive enough to have one labeled Over-and-Done-With.

7.

MISCELLANEOUS WARNINGS

Thursday, May 13, 2002

8:59 A.M.

I know Mary Matalin isn't calling from the West Wing just to entertain me, but whatever her nanny question is *this* time, I'm on high alert.

"Barbara, do you have a minute? I swear you will not believe this."

Make that *really* high alert—say, a three-alarm fire.

"I've got Ariel Sharon on one side of me and Prince Abdullah of Saudi Arabia on the other side. We're in the middle of the Middle East crisis and this place is *tense* . . ."

Let me guess. Her nanny calls.

"Then my nanny calls."

Working Washington Parent Rule Number One: *The nanny's calls are always put through.* Mary has never complained about

Penny before, so I assume the young woman interrupted her boss at work for a good reason. "Was one of the girls sick?" I ask. "Was Penny sick?"

"No, I guess it was even more urgent than that," Mary says with her signature biting sarcasm. "She wanted to know if the dry cleaner's could pick up her cleaning along with ours."

I'm about to say *You're kidding.*

"I absolutely kid you not. I told Penny she could call me *any time,* but I assumed she knew I meant *for an emergency.* So what do I do with this?"

Then I find out that Mary and James have been less than thrilled with their nanny, almost since I placed her with them a year ago. The whole story spills out: The nanny not only dressed like J-Lo around the house but she dressed the girls in clothes that could have come straight from Juicy Couture.

I thought Penny was right for the job: young and zippy, a strong enough personality to handle the energetic Matalin-Carvilles. But then there was the risk of all these dynamos colliding, which is what had happened.

Mary had never once complained, so I'd had no idea things weren't going at all well.

It's clear that Penny needs to go, on several counts. Mary and I both assumed she had a good grip on reality until we found out she didn't. Who knew she couldn't distinguish between World War Three and a dry-cleaning crisis? So I'm flipping out.

"Do you want me to talk to her?" I ask.

"I'll take care of it," Mary tells me cheerily. Maybe because her world is filled with real crises instead of imaginary ones, Matalin is a client who has things in perspective. I promise to find her another nanny as soon as possible.

. . .

So a nanny who seems like a star can be full of surprises, even after careful interviews and thorough reference checks. Holly was a clean, scrubbed North Dakota girl, not exactly refined, but solid working-class and thrilled with the terrific job I'd found for her. She was a wonderful multitasker and got four children to school, cleaned the house, and carpooled them to tutors and swimming lessons.

But some of Holly's friends started arriving to pick her up on motorcycles. In her spare time, she managed their band, and her outfits went from farm-girl prim to downright salacious. She made quite a splash in high-heeled python cowboy boots and a micro cowgirl skirt—at her employers' dinner party.

But Holly cleaned like a demon and was amazing with the boys. She even improved their baseball skills so all four boys made their teams. The parents were laid-back, and they felt that Holly's skills outweighed her deficits. Until the boys saw her in bed with the lead guitarist. Holly had forgotten to pull the curtains on her ground-floor room. (She thought the kids were deeply immersed in their homework. And they *were*.)

Even though sex ed is supposed to begin at home, I don't think these parents had this scenario in mind.

Today's mail includes an application from an eleven-year career nanny ready for her next assignment. Jocelyn's "Position Profile" states that she **will not** *work with parents who stay home,* **will not** *do heavy housework or parent-related errands, and* **will not** *work weekends, vacations, overtime, or for emergencies.*

Jocelyn sounds as if she's been talking to the nanny union. I've placed her before, and I know she's excellent. But no one *else* will know she's excellent if they read her daunting, negative job specifications, so I'll have to help her fine-tune her résumé a little differently. This talent comes with the territory in the Capital of Spin.

"Why don't you say you *prefer a job with working parents,* and that *you don't mind light housekeeping?*" I gingerly suggest. "And maybe you should be willing to help out if there's an emergency."

I turn on the air-conditioning, drink my already-warm iced coffee, and check my messages.

Every successful placement is unique, and so is every failure; there are short stories with happy endings, and there are less happy, long, *long* stories. Some relationships take months to blossom and go on for years. Some crash and burn as soon as the nanny is out of the gate.

So I'm always training for this job. One of these days I'll write a how-to-run-a-nanny-agency textbook: Screen clients carefully *before* sending them an application form. Pick up every clue you can and pay attention to your first impression. If a parent asks about my agency and then cuts me off in mid-sentence to take a more important call, I already know the children aren't her first priority.

"Can you help me?" is a good opening line. It's better than being barked at, as if there's no time for civility. Can I work with these parents, and trust them with one of my nannies?

Parents are evaluating me as well, of course. When Anthony Rich, the well-known investigative reporter and brand-new father calls, I brace myself for the firing—or should it be hiring?—squad. Rich is an authority on communication issues inside the CIA. His latest book is *everywhere;* I saw him this week on *60 Minutes* and *Letterman*. People I know in the news business tell me he's parsimonious and a real pain to work with, but I'm a sucker for a challenge.

Tony has to go on a forty-city book tour, and his wife is an equally absent parent, so they need about eighty hours of child-care a week in their northwest D.C. home. This sounds like at least *two* nannies to me, but I temporarily withhold that information. True to his reputation, he grills me. How long have I been in business? What criteria do I use to screen employees? What follow-through services do I provide? Are our nannies bonded?

And my favorite: Can they be discreet about their employers' private affairs?

No, not that kind.

Tony's asking some good questions, and I have the answers. I can handle him. When he finally starts to relax, he actually sounds charming. I'm exhausted when we're through, but this will be a go. Between him and Janette, my referrals from the media should generate a lot of great new business.

When a husband has been delegated the job of scouting out the nanny agency, he's often performing his due diligence as a new father. But sometimes, a call from the dad is a bad sign. I fall in love with him, and then, from the deep dark background, his wife emerges—the personality from hell. No wonder he was the front man.

"I'd like to talk to your wife," I tell him. Tony hasn't mentioned her yet, but I assume she is his child's mother and has some views of her own about what they need in a nanny. "Charlotte's a tax lawyer and just made partner at Loring and Howell."

He waits for me to acknowledge Charlotte's great importance.

"Since your wife's so busy, why don't you tell her to give me a call at *her* convenience?" Who wants to play tag with the likes of Charlotte?

Usually the fathers are a little tougher to talk to than their wives. But the mother is the make-or-break parent. He can tell me anything, but she's the major player.

When Tony's wife finally has a moment to call me, I find out who's the real investigative reporter in the family.

Inside of *one minute,* Charlotte Rich inserts three contemptuous insults into our first conversation. This is an all-time record. Didn't one of my nannies steal her employer's credit card? She heard that another White House Nanny quit a job after only three months into the placement. And was she the one who left in the middle of the night? I'm speechless.

"I honestly can't remember that," I say. I'm completely on the defensive. But once I regain composure, I'm *steaming.* My hard-earned integrity and reputation are being dragged through the mud.

"Let me stop you right there," I say after I mentally regroup. "If all these things are true, why are you calling me?" *I wouldn't want to work with me if I were you.*

"Oh, no." Charlotte puts on some very sudden charm. "We need a nanny *right away.* And I hear you're really good."

Why didn't she lead with that instead of the diatribe?

Needless to say, I'm not crazy about Tony's wife. I can't stand her long enough to work with her, so how can I subject one of my chosen women to her? Or her husband, when he forgets to be charming?

Dear Mr. and Mrs. Rich,
    The process of finding the right nanny is all about making a good match. Equally important to that process is finding the right

agency. After our recent telephone conversations, it is clear to me that we are not that good a match.

I'm returning your application and registration fee. I wish you success finding quality childcare for your family.

Good riddance. Whoops—Sincerely, BGK

After he gets my Dear John letter, Tony calls. "What did we do wrong?" he sputters, indignant. I'm slow to respond, so he adds, a bit softer in tone, "Was it my wife?"

You're damn straight it was your wife. Too bad I can't say that.

"I guess you could say it was a combination of factors," I say before we bid one another adieu. Calls fly back and forth during the following week until the Riches finally understand what "No" means.

Another placement I turn down is a journalist whose last nanny complained that the children were kickers and spitters, and that she had to work so many extra hours she was ready to escape. She's worked for this family for five years but is finally in a state of emotional meltdown.

When this mother calls, she begins with total disclosure. First she confesses she's run her own ad looking for a nanny and is beginning to understand that I earn my keep. Next she launches into a description of her children, including details about their psychological diagnoses as well as their intense sibling rivalry.

I'm starting to sink into my chair when she throws in the final detail: that this job is "really easy."

The job is really easy? I like this mother tremendously. But knowing the facts, how do I entice someone to take this job?

But assuming the prospective client hasn't set off any alarms, I always send them our application forms. And they often come back to us full of surprises. "Please don't send us someone religious. Our last nanny played Christian music while she drove our daughter to Temple for her bat mitzvah lessons." That's reasonable. Guess I won't send *that* client my Jehovah's Witness whose idea of an outing is taking the children for a walk through the neighborhood to drop off copies of the *Watchtower*.

One of my most memorable requests was from the parent of a student at St. Stephens–St. Agnes, a prep school in Alexandria commonly known as Stagnes: "I need someone, you know, young, attractive, well-dressed. I guess I mean, well, 'Waspy.'"

Did she really say that?

We get our share of "touchy" specifications like that. "My last nanny was from Africa and she didn't work out, so let's avoid that part of the world . . ."

One bad experience and they condemn an entire continent?

"I've heard nannies from [fill in the blank] are: messy, lazy, not punctual, unintelligent, too strict, too lenient . . ."

Or the other kind of erroneous generalization. "My friend has a fabulous nanny from Indonesia. Can we get someone from there, too?" *If this search is limited to the South Pacific, I hope you don't have a specific start date in mind.*

Nannies come with their own interesting biases. One turned down a position with a wonderful Bethesda family because, in her words, Jews eat too much tuna fish.

How did she know what I just had for lunch?

When parents send back their applications, many of them

seem to be on Information Overload. For instance, the "family sketch" I just received:

Susan is a Pisces. Her pet peeves are having to tell the nanny to do something rather than her taking the initiative. As a water sign, she's very sensitive to disorder. Roger is a Gemini; he's concerned about the Earth and his pet peeves are wasting food and wasting energy and resources (heat, light, water, electricity). Our daughter Ellie is a Leo, which means sudden flare-ups and tantrums. Also a Leo, Ellie's twin sister Maddie has a better disposition.

Twins with the same sign? I never could have figured *that* out.

I never know what the next bizarre challenge will be in this business, because there's always a new version of impossible-to-please out there. Did I say that's what makes my work interesting? It depends on the day you ask me.

Here are a few choice excerpts.

What specific skills and abilities are you looking for in a nanny?
Some requests are reasonable: knowledge of infant and child development, a good command of English, the ability to teach the child how to swim. Then there are the nanny fantasies: "She needs to speak (Finnish/Cantonese/Flemish/Catalan)." "We'd like a nanny with training in (gymnastics/figure skating/cricket/computer programming) . . ."

What is your policy on discipline?
This can be a revealing question. My favorite answer is a long explanation of how the parents plan to discipline the

nanny! Aside from the obvious "no-strike" rule, you'd be surprised how few parents have actually thought about the concept of controlling their children. If they told the truth, many of my clients would ask, *What discipline?*

Here's a verbatim excerpt (except for the child's name): "We're a high achieving family. Both of us are Yale Law graduates and the father clerked for a Supreme Court Justice, but we're *very* permissive with Annie. Eventually, she'll grow out of her bad behavior."

Along with all the basic questions, I ask clients for **Other Pertinent Information,** which is how I learn what I really need to know. Among the all-too-familiar favorite parent categories:

1. *The Slave Driver* uses the words "flexible hours." This is a bright-red-flag term. It means: "Our help is expected to work whenever and however long we want them." Paying overtime is not in the Slave Driver's vocabulary. Why do so many Washingtonians forget the law about a forty-hour work week?

   "Babies sleep a lot. Do I have to pay the nanny when the baby's sleeping?"

   No, but if you don't, the nanny might not be there when the baby wakes up. In other words, *there is no downtime.* They're paying for ten hours and they want their money's worth. If a child takes a nap, the nanny should be ironing the child's party dresses, bathing the dog, or making a soufflé for the family dinner. (I suggest they find a maid, a dog-sitter, and a chef. Then call me back.)

2. *The Analytically Inclined*
"Children need a lot of emotional space to express them-selves, and we expect our nanny to be comfortable with all their moods and forms of self-expression. Tiffany doesn't always like to wear clothes, so as long as she eats a balanced meal, we let her come to the table naked."

"We don't believe in rigid schedules. Our children sleep when they're tired and eat when they're hungry, so don't get caught up in conventional bedtimes or mealtimes."

"In order to reinforce Henry's self-esteem, we praise him as often as we can. If he's having trouble with his mul-tiplication tables, or making a snack, we encourage his independence by saying 'You can do it, Henry!' Even though it's tempting to make life easier for him, our son will be stronger and happier if he learns on his own. So let him make his own mistakes."

Does that include setting the house on fire?

3. *The Hyper-Vigilant*
"Never disarm the security system, even when you're home, and check all cabinet and toilet latches as well as safety gates at all times. Our children must not talk to strangers. Do not give our personal phone numbers out to anyone, and clear all personal visitors to the grounds or in the house with us first. Do not sort our mail or touch our trash. Our offices are off-limits to you and the children. Most important, even if others think you're be-

ing paranoid, let us know immediately if you sense anything *at all* is wrong with Richard or Jennie. Call us or
the doctor for even minor symptoms. We'd rather you
overreact than put them in harm's way. Don't forget the
#62 sunscreen!"

4. *The Harvard-Obsessed*

"Every moment of the day is a learning opportunity, from
the classical music on the radio to singing to our son in
your native language, or teaching him to play the piano.
Make use of our educational games and flash cards. Georgie
helps us count out change in stores and measure ingredients
for brownies. Please *read, read, read* him the intellectually
challenging literature we supply, and converse with him as
much as possible to improve his communication skills.
Television is limited to PBS channels 22 and 26, not to exceed a half hour daily. Don't let our youngest son watch any
television. Only Baby Einstein tapes."

5. *The Discipline-Phobic*

"Emily has a great deal of energy and needs to run free.
She's in a daredevil phase and experiments with risky behavior, so watch carefully when she walks on the table or
the kitchen counters. Please gently stop her if she bites you
or others, and make sure she doesn't play too vigorously
with her baby sister, or put marbles in her mouth. Explain
to Emily why her behavior isn't working and ask her to try
harder at cooperating. We don't believe in punishment or
time-outs. We never, *ever* use the word no."

And finally, beware **Miscellaneous Warnings**:

"Gareth needs to be reminded to use the bathroom as he can get distracted. Be alert to signals: jumping around if he needs to pee, or going to the basement or saying 'go away' if he needs to poop. There are occasional accidents, so if you are squeamish, please do not apply for this job."

If these overinformative parents spent as much time with their kids as it takes them to write such meticulous, exhaustive notes, they could certainly cut down on their nannies' hours. But even if the above excerpts sound forboding, these nanny-family unions can be harmonious and long-lived. Life is chaotic in any home, even when the parents are around, but I'm usually impressed by how well our nannies help raise—sometimes almost *entirely* raise—Washington's secret children.

8.

PANDAS AND NANNIES IN THE FAMILY WAY

To GIVE YOU AN IDEA of the troubleshooting *normally* involved in my business, here's a rundown of a recent day:

9:45 A.M.
Karen, who helps with our temp agency in the next room, is constantly running back and forth with questions and answers, so we debrief each other and regroup many times an hour. "Do we have someone who can work three days a week until September? Do we have a family who won't mind a nanny with a ferret, a nose ring, and a tasteful tattoo?"

A fairly hysterical mother of three calls from the home she just moved into this morning in Kalorama, a moneyed neighborhood of grand Edwardians and embassies. "We flew in last night from New Jersey and my husband left for his office at Homeland Security at five A.M. I'm sitting here in an empty house with a hundred cartons and three miserable kids. Thank God I had your number. I can't even find the crib."

I know the house is empty because I can hear the echo. "Let me get to work on this," I say as reassuringly as I can when I have no idea whether I can help or not. Even though I can't believe the woman didn't call us sooner, she sounds in such dire straits that my heart goes out to her. Karen and I both start searching for a temporary miracle worker for her—*stat*. I even try to think of a nanny we can *borrow* from someone for a few hours.

10:07

A nanny we placed with a couple in North Arlington calls in a panic from a neighbor's house. The nanny had locked herself out of the center-hall Colonial and, as if that wasn't bad enough, the toddler in her care was still *inside*. Our second emergency and it isn't even a full-moon Friday.

"Call your employer," I say.

"I was going to," she says, so frightened she can hardly speak. "But her unlisted phone number at the Department of Defense is *inside the house*."

Too bad she can't get the toddler to find the number and make the call himself. Okay. Now *I'm* hysterical. The mother of the locked-in toddler *would* have to work for Defense. This is not a phone call I want to make, but I have to find that number and use it—*immediately*.

"Oh, dear," says the mother I was afraid to talk to. "That happens all the time, so Sam's used to it. Just tell Nanny the key is in the barbecue. I should have mentioned that to her." I thought this client would give me an earful about my incompetent temp babysitters, but she was surprisingly pleasant and almost blasé about the situation, much to my relief.

And when I call the nanny back, she's also calm. "Oh, things are much better now, Barbara. Sam just crawled through the doggie door." She thanks me for the info about the key in the barbecue and hangs up.

If I'd known the child was a miniature Houdini, I wouldn't have bothered to panic.

10:30

Miscellaneous, more normal troubleshooting: I convince yet another partner of yet another law firm that he cannot cross out the "no-refund" clause in our contract. This takes me a half hour. At the rate he charges, I should have just earned two hundred and fifty dollars. *Note: ask my lawyer if I can institute billable hours when I talk to attorneys.*

When I look up, I see a very sweet nanny who's been working for one of my families for the past few years. She called yesterday to warn me she needed to come in and talk, but of course I forgot.

"Are you as miserable as you look?" I ask, putting my arm around her.

"Joanne has a seriously troubled kid but she won't deal with it," Danielle blurts out. "I like Jason, but he's so out-there-ADHD. He's out of control and refuses to do anything you ask him. He called me a bitch right in front of his mother and all she said was, 'Jason's just going through a phase.'"

Children go through phases when they're two, or four.

At ten, Jason has gone from one difficult phase to the next; his nanny loves him, but she's cracking from the strain. This mother can't step up to the plate, I guess because she's clueless when it comes to dealing with a small problem which has now become a very large one.

"You've got to sit down with Joanne and tell her she has to back you up when Jason gets out of line," I advise Danielle. If she wasn't about to get married and leave this job anyway, poor Danielle would have walked out on Jason by now.

And I wouldn't blame her.

11:45

I'm trying to find the time to comb my hair and put on lipstick. A gracious client named Alexa Trudeau has invited me to lunch and I'm actually dressed up for the occasion. Nannies and clients send me lovely thank-you notes, and sometimes flowers, but an upscale lunch will be a rare treat and I'm determined not to be late.

I'm excited to finally get to Charlie Palmer's, where Washington insiders congregate for lunch. A table near the window gives you a commanding view of the Capitol building. I've known Alexa's father-in-law Jim Trudeau's family for years, and I found nannies for him and his first and second wives. Jim the real-estate mogul is a known Washington entity and has been a great PR agent for me for years. So of course his son Alan's wife, Alexa, called me as soon as she became pregnant. She wants to get to know me. What a great excuse to escape my office. It's totally exciting to eat in a buzzing, celebrity-sprinkled restaurant instead of at my desk.

"I know you'll find us the best nanny in town," Alexa

says. We bond over the seafood pyramid, and after sharing the chocolate hazelnut tower for dessert, we hug good-bye like old friends. I love the idea of helping out a new generation of Trudeaus.

I have no idea this is a lunch I'll end up paying for.

3:10

I'm ready to face my world again. The next call is from Suzanne, who seems like one of the nicest law partners I've ever worked with. She's home on maternity leave with her two-month-old and seems a bit overwhelmed. We still haven't finished talking about what she's looking for in a nanny because every time she calls, she panics and hangs up because, *"Ohmygod, Alexander's crying!"*

Some women can talk to me and calm down their babies at the same time. And all I can hear from Alexander is the tiniest whimper. But I forgive Suzanne's hysteria. First-time mothers often feel this anxious and incompetent. And she's used to negotiating with very different, slightly more mature adversaries at her upper-crust national law firm.

"I'm getting good at this," Suzanne reports every time she calls me back. "I'm really a good mother."

"I'm sure you are," I answer every time she repeats her mantra. I'm utterly convinced this placement will be a shoo-in. "By the way, Suzanne, what did you think of the nannies I sent you?" Delmy from El Salvador and a lovely Brazilian woman named Rita are both wonderful candidates, experienced with babies and highly recommended. I assume Suzanne has at least called them for interviews by now.

"I'm *so* sorry. I just haven't gotten around to them yet. Actually, I'm calling to see if you have anyone else."

"I sent you my two top picks." Suzanne is engaging and pleasant to talk to, but I'm starting to wonder if we're on the same page. I can place either of these nannies in a heartbeat. *So what's taking her so long to call them?*

"If you decide these two won't work out for you, I can send a few more," I tell her. Good nannies have very short shelf lives around here, and if I didn't like Suzanne so much I'd let someone else interview Delmy and Rita immediately.

"I'll make those calls right away," she says before hanging up. It must be time to burp little Alexander again.

Things hum along for the rest of the afternoon. In fact, my day ends so gracefully I actually leave on time. Maybe I can walk my geriatric miniature schnauzer, Willy, before he leaves me a gift on the living-room rug.

The next morning, I find out I missed Janette Huntington's call. Things have been quiet on Wilton Road for the last several months. The nanny mentioned that Janette and David eat like rabbits, which means they eat fresh vegetables, but maybe Donna's adjusted to the South Beach diet by now. Janette gets teary when she kisses tiny Spencer good-bye before dawn, the nanny tells me. David's over the moon about his son, but he isn't home much to enjoy him.

I find out that they had at least one quality family afternoon together when I flip on the weekend news; Janette and her family are at the National Zoo, where Mei-Mei, the artificially inseminated Chinese panda, has just had her baby.

But when I hear Janette's message, there's urgency in her voice. The woman who so calmly reports national calamities must have one of her own. I brace myself and make the call.

"Thanks for getting back to me." Janette's walking across the tarmac, about to fly to New York with the President. She calmly announces her shocking sound bite in true newsbreak style: SADDAM CAUGHT, ANTHRAX FOUND—

"Barbara! MY NANNY'S PREGNANT!!"

"Donna's pregnant?" I gasp, trying to sound calm.

"It could be worse. She just found out, and she isn't due for seven months. She says she can stay until we find someone else." Janette answers my questions before I have time to ask them. "She *has* been grazing a lot in the kitchen, even in the middle of the night, but I just thought she needed the extra fuel to keep up with Spencer. Who knew she was eating for two?"

Was that panda story a foreshadowing?

I don't tell Janette that her dilemma is actually *mild* compared to another pregnant-nanny story. My neighbors, very bright people, hadn't noticed any change in their large Minnesota farm-girl nanny. Then she called them from Holy Cross Hospital to say she needed some time off.

"Were you in an accident? Are you all right?" my neighbors asked.

Their nanny said she was fine. And she didn't want visitors. Talk about hardworking, oblivious parents: Those employers had somehow failed to notice that their live-in nanny was—I kid you not—pregnant with twins.

So things could be a lot worse for Janette and David.

K aren and I go on high alert, searching our desks and files, calling in all our chips. The pregnant-nanny story has caught us off-guard. I've got Nancy and her Nanny Nation staff feeling sorry for me as well. I have to send Janette at least two nannies to interview as soon as possible so she'll calm down.

Janette interviews Kim first, and she likes her enough to hire her right away, but unfortunately, the feeling isn't mutual. Despite her impressive history in childcare, Kim is now on a new career path, studying computer science. Her classes start at six-thirty three evenings a week, and there's no way Janette can accommodate that schedule.

The next nanny I send Janette is *smitten* with the job—a little too smitten, unfortunately. Mindy the communications major asks Janette all about her career and hardly mentions Spencer. Did she think she was interviewing for a reporter position instead of a job as a six-month-old's constant companion? Another case of identity confusion. I see it all the time.

Even though Janette has hired me to find her a new nanny, she confesses that she went into high gear and put the word out on the street. Then she was bombarded with so many candidates, some not even legal, that she realized it was becoming her full-time job. Just when I can tell she's getting frantic, Karen comes into my office wearing a good-news smile.

Emma McBride's on the phone.

One of my favorite nannies ever. "Emma!" I shout, praying she isn't just calling to say hello and thank me again for her job. And—do I deserve this luck?—the family I placed her with a few years ago is moving to Chicago.

Sometimes that revolving District door works in our favor.

Janette deserves the luck, too. Emma's as charming as Julie Andrews in *The Sound of Music*. Back in England she was in something called Queen Alexandra's Royal Army Nursing Corps, which sounds impressive. Most important, Emma's employers have said more than once that she's magic with their baby and their toddler.

. . .

Emma's British, but she's been working in D.C. for five years so she knows her way around town," I tell Janette. "She already belongs to the Spring Valley nanny network." I can tell she doesn't quite get the significance of this, so I explain that Emma would be Spencer's entrée to the playground in-crowd.

"Did you say she's from England?" Janette interrupts my rave review. "Is there anyone else I should meet?"

I get it. Janette hasn't recuperated from upper-crust, unbearable Mrs. Plumb.

"Emma's a *totally* different model," I say. "Children adore her. By the way, I hear she can drive a tank."

"So she can certainly handle the Volvo," Janette laughs.

It's nice to be trusted, and two interviews later, the deal is signed.

And this time David doesn't mess around with my contract.

Despite everything I've done to find Donna's replacement, in the end I have to admit that astonishing luck has delivered her.

9.

A TWINGE
OF ENVY

AFTER EMMA is happily settled into her DKNY-decorated suite on Wilton Road, she sends me pink gerbera daisies with a note: *Thanks for this great job! Love, Emma.*

Thank God she doesn't seem to mind those smallish closets, maybe because Emma's so excited about the pool table. She's apparently pretty good at the game, and she wins tournaments whenever she gets the chance. Janette never mentioned the mahogany-paneled billiard room, but I'm sure she and David don't spend much time in it. Maybe Emma's talent will rub off on Spencer, as soon as he can hold on to a cue.

"Spencer's in love," Janette tells me, probably from the press section of Air Force One. "She's got him on an actual schedule already. And she's so flexible about her hours. David and I are both under the gun. I promised I'd cut back once we had the baby. But that was before 9/11."

She mentions a story about a shake-up in Homeland Security, which could mean two minutes and thirty seconds on air instead of her normal minute-twenty. She has to fit motherhood moments into her schedule like sound bites. And Stevenson, Schwartz and Witherspoon—especially their software clients all over the Pacific Rim—own David's existence.

He likes to feel invaluable to the firm, and the travel has always felt stimulating and heady. Worth all the jet lag and the discombobulation that come with the far-flung territory. Janette complains about David's schedule, even though she doesn't spend much more time with Spencer than he does.

Janette has her eye on even better stories. All she has to do is keep up her impeccable style. And live down the baby thing, the question mark hovering over her career right now. The network executives have to know she's still all theirs, despite that small maternal sideline.

The real truth is that Janette relishes every stolen moment with Spencer more than all her on-air glories put together. When he pulls himself up and wobbles around the living room, his laughter fills her heart. Would she enjoy him so much if she had to feed, bathe, diaper, dress, and play with him *all the time*?

David manages to squeeze in some superior daddy-time when he finally gets home. Even if he's in a crying jag, Spencer always breaks into a smile when he sees his dad, and Emma's finally off the clock. A nanny named Angela, who worked for another attorney dad, told me a very different story. "Mr. Stevens is supposed to relieve me at seven o'clock so I can eat and get to class," Angela complained. "But he sneaks into the house through the garage and locks himself in the bedroom. He thinks I don't see him. *Can you believe he's hiding from his own kids?*"

Unfortunately, I can.

A mother can work full-time—*outside the home,* to be politically correct—and raise wonderful children, even three or four of them. But she has to master that infamous *balancing act* about which so much has been written. And just like in the circus, some acts are more daring than others.

I see the entire spectrum of nonstop working mothers, from eighty-hour-a-week tightrope-walkers to the acrobats who stay closer to the ground. Some of my clients do slow down to mommy-track speed, and some even step down to "part-time" positions, but many of those would qualify as full-time beyond the Beltway. I've even placed nannies in the homes of non-working mothers. But they were as busy with their *lives* as they would have been with jobs.

We do have our small share of District moms at leisure. "I don't want a nanny who'll resent me if I'm lounging by my pool and she has to watch the children," a Potomac mother mentioned. She had enough time on her hands to alphabetize her children's toys and wanted them kept that way.

Some of these full-time moms make time to "chat" on various District mothers' websites, certainly a great way to exchange all the vital information one needs these days. Hardworking mothers (outside the home) also find time to connect with their peers all over the city—and even the world. I only talked to my friends and my mother.

I log in myself once in a while out of professional interest, and it's fascinating: doula recommendations, child-friendly New York restaurants, even support groups for moms with low-weight toddlers. My favorite latest posting: "Helppp! My four-year-old loves guns."

And I'm sure someone out there had a brilliant answer.

Janette and David are so used to *hectic*, they're sure life is supposed to be this rushed. Spencer is changing from minute to minute, and they're missing milestones every day. But their equally time-starved friends with children are all in the same boat.

Janette and David's ten-month-old and their careers are absolutely worth the sacrifice on both ends: cramming their home lives into moments. As I watch Janette each evening on television, I imagine the crawl lines at the bottom of the screen: *More troops to Afghanistan . . . bin Laden on the run . . . Spencer learned to use a spoon today and is already cruising around the room . . .*

In the end, it doesn't seem as if that much has changed for Janette and David since they've become parents. They've never had much downtime. Their Supernanny is devoted to their child and knows exactly what he needs at every minute. They can concentrate on work. Family togetherness is rarer than a Japanese cherry tree in bloom in Washington.

In January.

Unfortunately, David's mother isn't quite as satisfied with the situation. Jane Wilder stayed home on the north shore of Long Island to take care of her four children (with a lot of help from nannies and housekeepers), while her husband commuted to Wall Street. "I was sure Janette and David would be home by now,"

Grandma always says when Emma answers. "Does the baby ever get to see his mother?" she vents to the nanny, never questioning her son's absenteeism. "Have you tried those recipes I sent you, Emma?" Jane would like her son to eat home-cooked meals, and since Janette's a lost domestic cause, she assumes that's Emma's job.

Women's Liberation seems to have passed Jane by, since her idea of family life is a retro 1950s fantasy. Her career goal was raising four prestigious children and then resting on her laurels. She brought hot chocolate to David's hockey games and attended twenty-five years of recitals, tournaments, matches, and performances. Men are supposed to be driven and absent. Servants are meant to serve invisibly, remaining in the shadowy background. Children need their mothers. When Spencer's older, Jane will be shocked to see so many nannies at his soccer games. White House nannies bake birthday cakes, take their charges trick-or-treating, and help them buy Mother's and Father's Day presents.

Nannies who work for divorced parents are often even more central to the children's lives. Take Moira from County Clare who takes care of single-dad Bruce Madison's two little girls. Madison lives on an actual estate in McLean, Virginia, the Republican haven of Dick Cheney, Colin Powell, and Kenneth Starr. Moira adores the three- and five-year-old girls, and her generous salary helps her tolerate their workaholic father.

When Congress downsizes the federal payroll, it outsources a great deal of work to consultants like Madison. He was a domestic-policy adviser to President Reagan, and then he jumped into the private sector by starting his own lobbying firm. Working for the government *outside* the government can equal stratospheric federal contracts.

Snobby, old-time Washingtonians consider Madison nouveau D.C. riche and mock his taste in art, but I doubt he cares. He had his girls with wife number two, but one of his young researchers (an expert in infrastructure protection) eventually lured him away.

"Lisette is horrible to the girls," Moira tells me. Bruce's girlfriend sounds like the snooty, two-faced baroness in *The Sound of Music,* the character who tries to snag Captain Von Trapp away from Maria. The children are simply in her way.

"I can't believe he's getting serious about her. The dry cleaner told me it's a sure sign the girlfriend will soon be moving in now that she's sending him Prada instead of her usual Banana Republic." Like any sharp journalist, Moira knows how to find good sources to predict the future of a story. If this nanny decides to keep a journal, she could be on her way to the next Nanny Lit *New York Times* best seller.

"Bruce asked me to buy the girls' Christmas presents," Moira reports a few months later. "He had time to go to the Tiny Jewel Box for Lisette's diamond earrings, but I had to fight the crowds at Child's Play to get a zillion gifts for the girls."

This dad may be brilliant, but his nanny can see the disaster in his future and he's blind to it. She actually overheard Lisette suggest that Bruce start thinking about sending his girls to the right boarding school, "to give them every advantage in life."

"Do you believe she wants to ship his daughters out? She's got him hypnotized." Apparently, Lisette acts sweet to the girls when their dad's around; she brings them gifts and plays the doting stepmother-to-be. But the minute Bruce leaves the room, the girls don't even exist. "I can see right through her facade," Moira says. "I thought Bruce was supposed to be *brilliant*."

Alas, the perceptive nanny can't do anything but watch her employer self-destruct with another wrong woman. Her mission is to protect his children, and she takes it seriously.

. . .

Most of us in D.C. get our local gossip from the *Post* Style section's "Reliable Source." But for the most interesting D.C. intelligence, you have to consult the Nanny Mafia, whose members gather in Turtle Park, or at the Leland Center. The story of the Climbers—as in Social—demonstrates their invisible grip on this city of power politicos.

Mr. and Mrs. S.C. have a three-year-old daughter and are pregnant with their second child. They absolutely have to have "a certain kind of nanny." I assume this means someone who'll love and take great care of their children.

I offer them Teni from Ethiopia, Silvia from Italy, and Cecelia from Ghana, but the mother's not interested in interviewing any of them. I then come up with Aminata from Nigeria, who's a total whiz with babies and can multitask like crazy. I'd almost have another child just to hire her myself.

Caroline Climber doesn't go for any of my choices. Not even a nibble. "Our last nanny had wonderful nanny friends in our neighborhood, and all the children played together," she sighs wistfully. After investigating further—via the nanny grapevine— I find out that little Julia's playgroup consists of Clinton Administration insiders' children *only*. Just like birds of a feather, nannies and children of Important Democratic Families flock together. Jockeying for social standing in Washington starts *way* before preschool.

So the Climbers can maintain their social cachet, I have to find them a nanny who this obviously exclusive group will accept as one of their own. If Julia's nanny has the right friends, then so will Julia—and so will Julia's parents.

I finally get it. This placement is all about swing-set status, which will lead to bigger and better things. So I find them Hillary; not only can she handle a toddler and a new baby, but these days she happens to be dating a Senator Kerry staffer. Now the Climbers are *euphoric.*

Then Hillary calls me, very upset, a few weeks later. "I can't keep this job," she whispers.

"Has anything bad happened?"

"No."

"How have they treated you?" I ask her.

"They seemed really nice at first, but now she's questioning everything I do. I don't think she trusts me. The other nannies warned me about this. They say she'll nitpick me to death and he's cheap. I just can't stay here."

Whether any of this is true or not, the Climbers' former nanny has turned this local Mafia against them forever, and Hillary's ready to pack her bags. They should have picked Teni or Silvia after all because now they've fallen all the way down the Democratic social ladder.

Janette and David are secure enough to have made a better nanny choice, but this is one couple who could certainly keep *two* nannies busy. Janette has to work harder than her male counterparts so her bureau chief will notice her. The first-string reporter goes to Europe with the President while she still gets the "body watch" stories: the President riding a tractor, the First Lady at a school library. Anything for face time.

Even with Emma's superb help, they're both devoured by their careers plus the added responsibility of parenthood. When was the last time they even saw a movie? Have they turned on their new plasma TV?

David has always wanted to be a father, when he's home to notice; he's glad to pick up the slack and even cooks when he has to and doesn't complain about diapers. According to Emma, when David calls from far away, he always asks to talk to Spencer so he can listen to him gurgle. He hears Spencer cry at night before Janette does and tries to calm the baby down so she can get her three hours of sleep. But when Janette leaves for Andrews Air Force base at three A.M. and David's talking to someone in China in the middle of the night and Spencer has an earache, Emma's their safety net. She's worth her weight in gold, which is just about her monthly salary.

It's a good thing both these parents are earners. But Janette doesn't work this hard in her brutal business *just* for the money. High-profile women correspondents usually step down to magazine shows after they have children, but that's not Janette's vision. She digests a daily mountain of newspapers, magazines, newsletters, e-mails, and faxes as well as every hundred-page White House document the press secretary throws at her.

She relishes her relentless calling, but her passion for Spencer is just as demanding. *I can do this,* she reminds herself. I hear that mantra all the time, but not every mother who says it writes a lead for the morning news while coaxing her infant to sleep for the fourth time—at two A.M.

Wednesday is Emma's "early" day (to make up for all those late ones). Janette works all afternoon on a story she really cares about: the Education Reform Act. Raising our nation's literacy rates, she says, is "a passion shared by Democrats and Republicans alike."

It takes longer than usual to write an open-and-close for her live shot from the East Room, so she calls Emma to apologize. "Not to worry," Emma tells her. "I was only going to go to the gym." Janette, who can't function without her personal trainer, knows how important it is for her nanny to stay relaxed and in shape. She feels guilty about this infraction, and she's afraid to promise it won't happen again. The good news is, her education story's in the top block to lead the evening news.

"Do I hear Spencer coughing?" she asks.

"He was so congested I raced him over to the pediatrician's office on Massachusetts Avenue right before they closed. But the medication is totally working," she says. "He's much better now."

Would I have dealt with this as well as she did? Janette wonders.

Just as she's packing her briefcase, the station manager taps her on the shoulder and tells her to stick around. Attorney General Ashcroft has declared an orange high-risk alert: possible terrorist attacks, timed to coincide with the first anniversary of 9/11. Janette's so tired she can hardly follow the details of the late-breaking story, and by the time she leaves the station, her much more important story has been killed. Striking fear in viewers is always a better sell than an in-depth story about substantive issues such as health care and the environment. If it bleeds, it leads.

She needs enough sleep to get through a White House press briefing early in the morning. Too wound up to relax, she orders golf clubs online for David's birthday and reads some government documents. If Janette could remember which hotel her husband's sleeping in this week, she'd fill him in about her awful day. But she'll have to wait for some sympathy. He's in the wrong time zone, anyway.

Janette hasn't seen Spencer since she kissed him good-bye, without waking him, at dawn. When she tiptoes past the pastel-striped nursery fifteen hours later, she notices Emma curled up on the daybed next to Spencer's crib, both of them in deep REM sleep. She's touched by this idyllic scene. Realizing what *really* matters, she's overcome with sweet emotions.

Next comes a twinge of envy.

Janette notices the huge stack of newspapers in the hall—which Emma was supposed to put out for recycling and now it's too late. By next week the house will be so full of old news they won't be able to move.

And why hasn't that pile of laundry been folded and put away?

What's wrong with this picture? Janette's on top of a rapidly spinning world and keeping her balance, not counting a difficult day now and then. She tells the rest of us what we need to know about almost everything.

But she's just a *little* envious of the woman who gets to sleep with her child.

10.

EVERY BIG RED DOG
HAS HIS DAY

ANY WORKING MOTHER who's away from her baby too
long envies the caretaker at one time or another, so I'm
not surprised when Janette's emotions get the best of
her. Another story, speech, document, or photo op always keeps
her working too late to get home before Spencer goes to sleep.
Sometimes she cajoles Emma into keeping him awake just a little
longer, but her nanny's probably right: When he plays with Mom
or Dad until all hours, he's a mess in the morning.

Think of the upside, she tells herself. *Every day of my life is different. I get to probe the power behind the throne. I walked through the
World Trade rubble with POTUS right after the towers fell.* Then
there's the downside. The *senior* correspondent goes to Spain, and
Janette gets the Western White House body watch, standing in
front of bales of hay and rusted farm implements in Crawford
just in case George Bush says something newsworthy. When she

went after this job, Janette assumed she'd be hanging out in a decent presidential retreat like Martha's Vineyard, Santa Barbara, or Kennebunkport, but no such luck: She gets East Jesus, Texas. Her makeup keeps melting and her bureau chief keeps calling for more news about No Child Left Behind.

Which is exactly what Janette is thinking about: Right about now, Emma's singing "Hush Little Baby" to her drowsy, left-behind child. In the fifteen-hundred-dollar chair she bought so she could rock him to sleep—herself.

What was she thinking?

Doing it all means being bombarded by every feeling in the book, including guilt, jealousy, and being upstaged by your nanny.

Which one client made sure never happened. I sent Claudia, a recent grad from a top-notch college, to what I thought was a dream job with a wealthy D.C. couple whose only discernible occupation was managing their investments. A butler, driver, chef, and housekeeper helped them and a four-year-old daughter get through their privileged days.

Claudia was ready to throw herself into her duties after the butler greeted her and introduced her to the child; when the mother woke up at noon, she took her child out for a three-hour lunch while Claudia waited around with nothing to do.

When they returned, the mother wanted to be left alone with the little girl. "I don't want Nanny to get in my way," Claudia overheard her tell the housekeeper. This client really wanted an invisible nanny, so Claudia quit.

That's an extreme example, but mothers do worry about being replaced by their children's caregivers. "What if my baby bonds with his nanny instead of me?" a client who works for

Fannie Mae asked me. "That's my biggest fear. I was home for three months, and just when my daughter was starting to recognize me, I was out the door." After another few months, this mother realized that the child loved her profoundly, just differently than she loved her nanny.

It takes time for parents to realize this, but my goal is always to make a match with that kind of comfort and confidence. Ultimately, I have to *intuit* who'll work well with whom. Some parents have actually asked for their prospective nannies' *astrological signs* to make sure they're compatible. But my application, personal interviews, and instinct still seem more reliable than the planets.

I pay very close attention to what my clients tell me.

"I'm not looking for a best friend," some announce up front. Translation: *I want our nanny to know her place.*

I remember a charming District family that ordered up a Knightsbridge model nanny, only to lock her in the basement and throw away the key. Their white-carpeted home was a showplace, but the nanny was relegated, with the children, to the lower quarters in true *Upstairs, Downstairs* style. At least they didn't expect the nanny to wear a uniform; when those requests come in, the employers usually mean the enlightened version: white shirts and khaki slacks.

"We want our nanny to be a member of the family," others say, all too endearingly. Beware. This can mean: *We expect her to love the job enough to do it for free.* "Our Bolivian housekeeper thanks God every day for putting her in our home," a well-known human-rights activist told me. After she described the sixty-plus-hour-a-week position, "plus flexibility on Saturdays," and the meager salary, I was tempted to inform the client (whom I had to turn down) that *human rights begin at home.*

What I'm always looking for at White House Nannies is the happy medium, when parents and nannies report that they're a great team. When parents work—*a lot*—it takes an efficient partnership to raise their children. This means communicating with their caregiver, *face to face.* E-mail, notes on the refrigerator, and phone calls don't always do the trick.

My high-tech parents call this exchange of information the download of the day; for the politicos, it's the debriefing: *By the way, we're out of diapers and, sorry, the car is in the shop so you'll have to put the little guy in the backpack and his brothers in the stroller and walk to the Giant. And while you're there, Jason needs more cough medicine. Call Dr. Korengold for a new prescription because the green stuff made Jason throw up last night. And I'm really sorry about this, but I didn't have time to wash his yucky sheets. I know I need to pay you, but I'm totally out of checks, so could you call the bank and order me some?*

Some D.C. parents have certainly mastered the art of the rhetorical question.

These exchanges of information occur during the "handoff" maneuver from parent to nanny. Some mothers can't wait to rush out the door as soon as their relief reports for duty, especially on Monday morning, so they keep it short and sweet: *I'll be in San Francisco until Wednesday and we're out of peanut butter.* Then there are the micromanager types who keep nervously running back into the house to tell their nanny one more crucial detail. *Did I remind you to wash the baby's laundry with Dreft?*

Some parents want to chat *at length* about every burp, bump, and B.M.—*after* they get home from work. On the *nanny's* time. Even though she's written up an hourly log. Some nannies are minimalists (*Ariel bit Jessica on the leg but I found the Band-Aids*), and some report every cute thing the child said and did and every-thing he consumed over the last ten hours.

Janette, David, and Emma are in the "great team" category. But even though things are going really well on Wilton Road, moods are bound to erupt, and not just Spencer's when he's teething.

David has been going through his own new-dad series of shocks. What happened to his sacrosanct Tuesday-night squash game at the University Club? When did grocery shopping be-come *his* job? Why can't he get to the dry cleaner's when it's open? *Couldn't Emma buy a few groceries and pick up his shirts on her way back from the park?*

But no matter how many chores a nanny takes on, the effi-cient time-managers I work with, most with billable hours, face an impossible daily challenge after they become parents. "I've never been so conscious of every second," said an overworked fe-male partner at Dickstein, Shapiro, Morin & Oshinsky. "I'm on my boss's clock, my clients' clocks, and my nanny's clock."

And what about the baby's clock?

Mothers who breast-feed need to pump enough milk so their nannies can feed the baby while they're at work, but even careful planning can fail. "While I was out for a quick errand on a Sun-day, the baby started to cry. My *clueless* husband couldn't stand the noise even for five minutes, so he calmed her down with some of the precious freezer stash I pumped to get us through the week. 'That's *liquid gold,*' I yelled at him. 'Next time, just hold the baby off until I get home!'"

It's all about strategizing, making the most of every minute and ounce of energy. "I set my watch ten minutes ahead," a lob-byist explained. "I know how many seconds it takes me to get to the elevator, to the lobby, to the car, through the parking gate, through rush-hour traffic, and over the bridge into Old Town. I've got it down to a science."

Like most of my female clients, Janette's passion extends way beyond the nursery—the State of the Union speech, for instance, and the President's Emergency Plan for AIDS Relief—which means less time with her child. She's eager to cover bigger stories than Laura Bush's Christmas at the White House. Any day now, her executive producer will realize Janette has more to say. At least he's already paid her *his* highest compliment: *I'd never even know you were a mother.*

All the glory pales when she sees Spencer take his first wobbly steps. When she tells David the big news, he says he's glad she finally noticed. Emma, of course, was smart enough not to breathe a word about Spencer's accomplishment. These missed magic moments break mothers' and fathers' hearts, and if the nanny sees the baby's first smile, or the first time he rolls over, sits up, crawls, gets a tooth, or babbles an actual word, she often keeps this information to herself.

Some days Janette has to fix her tearstained face before the six A.M. live shot. Congresswomen, judges, and multinational executives have confessed how terrible they feel when they hear instead of see their children's milestones, so I know how torn she feels.

"When I'm at work I pretend I don't have a family, and when I'm home I pretend I don't have a job," a litigator recently told me.

"My maternal instincts and my professional instincts are at war," said another seventy-hour-a-week attorney. "When you've worked a grueling ten-hour day while your nanny was at the preschool picnic, it's hard not to envy *her* career."

Who has the better job? Janette and her female colleagues who employ nannies ask one another frequently. As proof, read the endless supply of angst-ridden, why-am-I-working? postings on the various District mothers' websites: "My child runs to the nanny when he has a boo-boo, even if I'm standing there."

And how can I forget the couple who purposely hired an Ecuadorian nanny so their child would be fluent in Spanish? The plan worked so well that the nanny and their son were soon chattering away and the parents couldn't understand one word they said.

One mother, not the jealous type, told me about the night her son had an earache and called out for his nanny. "I want Elmira," he sobbed. His physician single mother had had a trying day herself. Unable to comfort her bereft child, she ended up wailing, *"I want Elmira, too,"* until they both fell back to sleep.

Many of my clients are routinely out of town, some out of the hemisphere, and they seem to thrive on the incessant, ramped-up demands of their impressive professions. But sooner or later, most mothers experience those moments when the grass looks greener at the playground.

Emma the seasoned nanny knows how to deal with these jealousy-prone situations. When Janette hears Spencer gurgle "Emma," one morning, her nanny assures her he was really saying *"Momma."*

Emma is thrilled with her current position, especially after several trials by fire with previous employers. One couple actually left her home with their three young children while they went on a month-long European holiday.

"It was all right," the always-chipper Emma explains. "They came back from Paris one weekend to relieve me."

Emma's main complaint about her current job is the one I hear constantly from my nannies: When Janette and David get home later than they expected to, they keep Spencer up way past his bedtime. "I've got him fed, bathed, and calmed down, ready for a story, but instead of putting him to bed, they wind him up again. Last night they took Spencer to Chef Geoff's and he didn't go to sleep until eleven o'clock, so I had to deal with a cranky, miserable boy the next day."

I take Emma's complaint to heart. "If I have a problem with the kids," she says, "it's always the parents' fault." When my clients let their children stay up late, it's often because they can't figure out how to get them to sleep! I advise Emma to tell Janette and David that their child needs a regular, early bedtime routine.

"I'm happy to give Spencer his bath," Emma reports to me. "But I explained to Janette that bath time is precious, and that she should really try to be home in time for it."

Janette and David are so bonded to Emma, they can't imagine life without her, so they listen, and whatever their nanny says *goes.* In fact, any of Janette's new-mother friends could write her version of the book entitled *My Husband Ran Off with the Au Pair. Oh, How I Miss Her.*

As one mother put it, "I take better care of my nanny than my husband. If he leaves, I'll at least still have my job." A mother and father who both commute to New York tell me they couldn't function without their lifesaver nanny, Margie. "She remembers Jeremy's doctor's appointments and to have our gutters cleaned. She cleans whatever the housekeeper misses, and she organizes *everything,* from our file cabinets to our sock drawers. The night Jim and I both came home from terrible days at work, she'd set the table with flowers and cooked us *coq au vin.* Margie is our *wife.*"

By the way, this particular Supernanny is the very same one my financial mother (in Chapter Six) wouldn't hire because her abundant cleavage overshadowed her other attributes.

So in my business, the old adage is true: One client's trash is another's treasure.

Multitasking nannies are crucial these days, since mothers are faced with what has been called the "cult of Momism." As if Washington's women don't have enough achievement anxiety on the work front, their *other* job gets more and more demanding. They have to stay informed about the latest theories concerning their children's nutrition as well as their emotional, physical, and intellectual well-being.

When and how should I wean my infant? My toddler is beginning to read, but I'm worried that his gross motor skills are delayed. In addition to joining a Mommy and Me group, the well-informed D.C. working mom reads every book she can find about each stage of her child's life. She subscribes to parenting newsletters and web-sites. And she assigns this same reading to her nanny.

When Janette's finally in bed, after she's skimmed her notes on the day's press gaggle, she reads T. Berry Brazelton's *On Becoming a Family*. Everything about her child fascinates Janette, and she could easily spend another few hours reading D.C. Working Moms postings from all her equally sleep-deprived mothers-in-arms.

Sleep—for babies and their moms—is an enormous topic, and Janette has read enough to know that Dr. Ferber's help-your-child-sleep-through-the-night strategies have been modified by Mindell. And speaking of Ferber, I was sure I'd finally satisfied Suzanne Taylor, the attorney who was going to be an easy client. Boy, was I wrong! Suzanne never even interviewed those great nannies from El Salvador and Brazil.

"Do you have anybody *else* for me?" she asked. Every time she called—to reject another nanny—her baby squirmed or squealed or burped, and she suddenly had to hang up. She'd made partner at a major law firm, but choosing her nanny was obviously too daunting a task.

I pride myself on my ability to create good parent-nanny teams, but I couldn't get to first base with Suzanne.

I finally got Suzanne's unspoken message and sent her Mrs. Blakesly, the pearls-and-silk-blouse, matronly type (read *white*). It was love at first sight. Mrs. Blakesly was so clear about her mission, this highly insecure mother could finally relax; it seemed like the perfect partnership—until I got the hysterical call.

"She wants to *Ferberize* my baby," Suzanne shrieked into the phone. "Alexander was in terrible distress and she was just letting him scream."

"Oh, my God," I sympathized, with no idea what she was talking about. This was obviously an infant-development break-through, and I was out of the loop! As soon as I got off the phone, my assistant, Karen, informed me that Mrs. Blakesly was simply following Dr. Richard Ferber's advice to let the toddler cry long enough so he can learn to comfort himself, then fall asleep.

Clearly not the right method for *this* mother, who can't stand to hear her child whimper for one second.

Time to replace the competent Mrs. Blakesly.

As Spencer's birthday approaches, Janette throws herself into his party preparations; Emma's very excited about it, too, and as happy to help as always. Janette is thrilled that the party will be on her son's actual birth date. One of her White House correspondent colleagues was in Rome with Colin Powell on *his* child's first birthday, so they had the party a few weeks late.

This only works until the child is old enough to know his actual birth date.

Spencer's party theme will be Clifford, the currently *de rigueur* Big Red Dog. But when Emma tries to book the *actual* Clifford, she finds out he's on a national tour and unavailable. This is clearly a crisis: a tacky pretend-Clifford will be immediately sniffed out by the Spring Valley guests, especially those most discerning ones in diapers.

Janette is so desperate for the actual celebrity to appear, she convinces his publicist to add Spencer's birthday bash to the tour schedule. Who says a high-profile career isn't great for her child?

Emma orders the tent, the carousel, and a lavishly catered Occasions luncheon of field greens, grilled salmon, and Pinot Gris for moms and dads, and mini tofu doggies and bone-shaped spinach quichettes for the younger set. Emma—and therefore Spencer—has been socializing with all the right children, so Janette's guest list is impressive and the event is a huge success. Cell phones are only spoken into sub rosa, as this Saturday twelve-to-two slot is sacrosanct.

No one utters the "quality time" cliché anymore, but everyone still thinks it.

In the middle of lunch, while three of our most fun White House Nanny temp babysitters feed the children and the parents are in full-tilt networking mode, David evaporates to take a quick call from his Hong Kong office. Emma, who'd never miss Spencer's birthday party, even if she weren't being paid overtime, takes up the slack.

When Spencer blows out the giant candle on his Clifford cake and David is still gone, Janette begins to fume. She gives her husband a phony smile when he finally returns while she's passing out the children's goody bags: an organic Clifford cookie with their name in frosting, and a picture of each child with the Big Red Dog.

David was in charge of the parents' gifts: *Stupid White Men* by Michael Moore, and, to be fair to the minority guests, David Frum's *The Right Man: The Surprise Presidency of George W. Bush*. But even though he made sure to have the books autographed, Janette won't forgive him for his inexcusable absence. She worked overtime on the party and he missed more than half of it. While Emma helps Janette and David straighten up the house, she feels a storm coming on.

"This was a moment you can never recapture," Emma hears Janette inform her husband in a frozen voice.

"*I had no choice,*" he tells her. "Unfortunately, no one in China cares about Spencer's birthday."

"Does that mean *you* don't care?"

This is the last thing Emma hears before rushing off to the Irish Pub for some pool and beer.

11.

GOOD NIGHT, (DYSFUNCTIONAL) MOON

THE SMALL, occasional squabble on Wilton Road is *nothing* compared to the marital strife some of my nannies have witnessed. A former Presidential adviser was so upset about his wife's extravagance that he dramatically cut her credit card in half, right in front of the nanny, who told me all about it. And to make matters even more awkward, the nanny still had *her* family credit card for child-related expenses.

That highly placed dad didn't realize he had as much going on at home as he did at the White House. His wife loved to cuddle her baby in bed while he drank the baby formula—and she drank hers: Jack Daniel's. I guess she didn't want to leave the six-year-old out of the fun, because she told the nanny to give him more Ritalin than the doctor had prescribed.

No nanny wants to work in a danger zone, but unfortunately some of them have to. A young nanny from California first realized she'd moved in with an *unusual* family when she heard the biotech executive mother put her children to bed via intercom: *"Lizzie and Carter, get into your jammies."* Then five minutes later she trilled: *"Nighty night. Mummie loves you."*

Next, the nanny was awakened before dawn by shattering glassware and screaming. Terrified, she called her father in San Francisco, who said to stay in her room until it was time to report for duty.

"You may have heard a little noise this morning," the father (a master of understatement) mentioned casually when she arrived in the kitchen to prepare the children's breakfast. A smashed crystal bowl was still all over the floor. "Nothing to worry about. *This* time I got Helen's performance on video. I'll let her buy the tape back from me, but I'm sure she'll be on her best behavior from now on."

If his threat doesn't work, I'm sure the video will come in handy for the custody battle in court.

That nanny didn't ask me to find her a new job until *two years* after the domestic *Kristallnacht.* Even when a family sounds like *The War of the Roses,* the nanny is often so bonded to the children, she chooses to stay. Another devoted nanny working under difficult conditions returned from a weekend off to find the mother crawling down the hall, bandaged from neck to waist and writhing in pain. The woman, who'd obviously had recent surgery, called the pharmacy for more painkillers because her prescription had run out.

A few hours later, the nanny and the children heard the mother begging her anesthesiologist husband for more drugs. After he refused, she swore a blue streak at him. "You're the one who wanted the tummy tuck and the boob job," he shouted. "Now live with it!"

What should a nanny tell a child who doesn't understand why his parents hate each other?

One crazy week, we wondered if there was an anger epidemic around here. One dad needed a nanny *fast* because his wife was suddenly, mysteriously *gone*. "Looks like I'll be a single parent for a while," the father of three told me.

Divorce? Illness? Had she been called to active duty in Iraq?

"How long are you going to need someone?" I asked. He wasn't exactly sure. The mother had been court-ordered from the house and was living somewhere else. "I told the children Mommy's in time-out," this government attorney explained. I sent him a wonderful nanny named Maggie, but the troubled seven-year-old girl was a piece of work. "You're not the boss of me," she told the nanny, throwing toys and tantrums.

Maggie apologized for using our emergency line and waking me up out of a sound sleep, but she definitely had a problem. The little girl had called her mother and said the nanny was hurting her. The frantic, banished mother called the neighbor, who called the police. Maggie called the father, and he called the grandparents. Cars arrived at the house from every direction, turning that peaceful suburban Maryland street into a scene straight out of *Cops*.

Angry children are hard enough to deal with; smart angry children are even harder. Mom wasn't the only one who needed a time-out in that family.

Dads lose it too, of course. A tax-attorney father of three, normally a wonderful, hands-on dad, was a bit *too* hands-on when he put his momentarily uncontrollable toddler daughter in the clothes dryer! And our nannies often have to take children to their sporting events because their dads have been yellow-carded for being overinvolved in their games.

One divorced dad hired a nanny whose bedroom was right

next to his, which was fine until he started dating. The first time he brought a woman home, the nanny suggested he conduct his social life when she wasn't around because the walls were evidently thin.

"Don't be silly," the dad assured her. "Nothing happened." After the next "date," the nanny confronted the dad again. *"But we didn't do anything,"* he protested innocently.

"Don't lie to me," the nanny said. "I'm the one who changed your sheets today." If he wanted to entertain at home, she suggested he could put her up in a hotel. It was cheaper to move the nanny to another part of the house.

It's no surprise that unbalanced parents tend to knock their children off-balance as well. A pair of attorneys were so competitive with each other that when she made partner and he was only lateraled to another firm, the atmosphere at home became as frozen as the Alaskan tundra. Their five-year-old talked to herself for long periods of time, the nanny reported, and the preteen son was already a substance abuser. When the school psychologist called, the parents blamed their children's teachers. The nanny was the only reliable, constant source of comfort in that family, and even though she adored the children, she finally asked me to find her another job.

"Why were those brilliant Ivy League law-review parents so out-of-control in their own home?" I asked her.

"They're such high achievers," she said, "they can't acknowledge any imperfection in their children."

I'm used to calls from executive assistants and household managers. But the first time a "life coach" called, for a woman named Alyssa who needed a *lot* of help running her own life, I could tell

I was in dangerous territory. The unpleasantly divorced woman's life sounded completely derailed. So—no surprise—both her children had serious "issues."

I followed my instincts and politely tried to take a pass.

But the life coach cleverly managed to seduce me into coming on board to help this desperate mother. I'm a social worker at heart, so I said I was willing to try as long as I could meet the client in person to evaluate her unusual situation. The mother, who never appeared before noon, was an hour late for our one o'clock appointment. The curvaceous brunette who was supposed to be running a multimillion-dollar real estate corporation was incapable of making eye contact. She was apparently such a world-class shopaholic that she kept one employee busy returning the results of her manic sprees at Bloomingdale's, where she sometimes spent $60,000 a day.

And in case you're wondering, she *was* scheduled for weekly therapy; the problem was getting her there.

"What kind of help do you think you need?" I asked.

"Well, the children need some structure," she said, even though she obviously didn't want any imposed on her. "And they're eating too much junk. I want someone to cook good food for them." After listening for a while, I realized that this client needed more than just childcare. Her work-related obligations kept her out late several nights a week at business dinners and the like. According to her life coach, she also had an active social life and needed to be driven home from Washington's finest watering holes in the wee hours of the morning. I suggested a live-in couple: a nanny/household manager as well as a driver.

The first couple I sent to this client was rejected. She was afraid the forty-year-old man might see her in a nightgown and find her irresistible. So I sent a wonderful couple in their fifties: a take-charge nanny and great cook, and her husband, a fine chauffeur and gardener whom one could hardly imagine being led astray by this siren of a mother.

"This is a hard job," I told them. I'd been warned that not only was the mother a handful, but the children were "a little challenging," although the details were vague. In their first week on the job, the younger child threw a rock and shattered the couple's car windshield; the older child made them drive her the two blocks to school. The mother was too busy to get to Back to School night, so she asked the nanny to go for her.

Despite the $125,000 salary and free apartment, my instincts had been right. The couple only lasted three weeks.

Undisciplined children are high on nannies' lists of complaints. In one Jamaican woman's words, "My bosses are too busy running down the mighty dollars to take control of their spoiled monsters." And all too often, after a nanny asserts some control over the children, the parents undermine her authority.

"If Jenny hits her brother, don't let her watch TV," the parents insist. After Jenny whacks her baby brother, the nanny turns off the television; but the parents can't stand her whining, so they turn it back on. "It's her favorite show," they explain sheepishly to the nanny. "We have to choose our battles."

Perhaps D.C.'s workaholic parents think giving their children total rein will make up for not spending enough time with them. It takes far more effort, of course, to control children than to give in to them—until you pay the enormous price later on. When one client's executive assistant called me to discuss adding a *third* nanny to her employer's staff, she mentioned that the family's chef always prepared several entrées for the children's meals: macaroni and cheese, hot dogs, pbj's, scrambled eggs, and chicken fingers, etc., so the youngsters could have their choice.

What ever happened to "Eat it or wear it?"

An elected official (who'll remain nameless) and his wife were so involved in their reelection campaign, they were clueless on the home front. When the nanny gave their child cereal and a banana for breakfast, he screamed for candy instead. The child howled so loudly that he woke his mother, who stormed into the kitchen.

After the nanny explained she was trying to get him to eat something healthy, the mother dumped a bag of M&M's into junior's bowl. "*Just give him the chocolate,*" she snarled, before turning on her bare heels and going back to bed.

No wonder nannies never last long in that household.

Parent applications often reveal the nanny will have discipline issues:

We don't believe in a critical or negative atmosphere. Please enlist Will's voluntary cooperation by offering him candy or a treat instead of issuing orders or setting boundaries.

We listen to what Amelia is trying to tell us, and we remain patient as she struggles to know her own needs, her own gifts, and her own soul. We think no is too *negative* a concept.

We try to sweeten things for our four-year-old. A boring errand is always followed by a trip to the park. If Mummy has an important meeting and will be too busy to play for a while, we ask what special toy Gracie wants us to buy for her. If she has to leave a fun activity before she's ready, we get her a Popsicle on the way home. So that child will go through life asking *Where's my Popsicle?*

Some parents belong to the Neville Chamberlain school of parenting: peace at any price. Imagine trying to find a nanny to take these jobs! Many of the nannies I place come from *functional* homes, so they're in shock when they encounter the other kind.

As one nanny passed a wall of framed family photographs while touring her prospective residence, she assumed this was the typical D.C. "wall of fame": pictures of the parents with various heads of state and foreign dignitaries. Then she realized she was staring at nude shots of her employers-to-be, in various exotic locations. They were an unusually "arty" couple for Washington, and their taste was obviously beyond that Montana nanny's comfort zone.

Also in the "unusual" category were the parents who mentioned that their house was haunted, but they reassured the nanny that their ghosts were friendly. Another couple told me fairies watched over their children when they were at work. Did that mean the nanny could spend her time walking the dog?

Jeffrey Darwin, alias Maserati Man, is certainly in this Slightly Weird category. He's the guy with the capacious McMansion and all the sports cars. Jeffrey and his wife have already been through two great nannies, so whenever he calls, I already know why.

Everyone in this town brags about what they do, but I still have no idea what Jeffrey actually *does* in one wing of his residence while his children and nanny are in the other wing. Besides call me. In fact, I've never even spoken to his wife. But she gave birth, so I assume she exists.

"Hello, Barbara," he says ever so sweetly. "Are you thinking about me?"

Jeffrey should only know that, yes, I definitely *am* thinking about him. Before I reveal what his very tolerant nanny told me, I need to explain some D.C. demographics: Virginia, the red state, usually means Conservative Republican, while my more liberal clients tend to live in blue Maryland.

The Darwins live in permissive, child-centered Potomac, Maryland, where they sleep with their three children in what's trendily called "the family bed." (Richard and I bonded with our children during waking hours because they slept horizontally and flapped their arms like windmills, and our sleep was too precious a commodity.)

"I can't take it anymore," the Darwins' latest nanny complained. "Jeffrey and June don't believe in alarm clocks, and the children are late for school unless I tiptoe into the parents' bedroom and get them up." That doesn't sound so terrible to me—until the nanny adds that the Darwins are still in that family bed—*naked*—when she has to fish the kids out of it.

The astonishing case histories never end. One nanny became so close to the family she worked for, her boss's brother assumed he could join her in bed. I'd staffed that house for years, so I was as shocked as my poor nanny when she called to say, "Get me out of here!"

And I knew I had made a mistake sending a young woman to work for a peculiar family in Cleveland Park, D.C. The husband ate dinner hunched over, his arms encircling his plate as if he was protecting his supper from predators. The child ate directly off her plate, like a dachshund. Neither parent said a word about the strange mealtime behavior.

When the nanny, aghast, couldn't stand it any more and suggested the child try using a utensil, the parents looked at her as if she were asking their daughter to walk on the ceiling. I can't believe that nanny lasted more than a day, but she lasted two.

But back to the refreshingly normal Huntington-Wilder household, where Emma's hardest challenge is her grueling schedule. She's on duty weekday mornings at seven, unless she has to start even earlier. She's free no later than eight P.M. *If* Janette or David happens to get home by then.

At first, she'd crawl downstairs and collapse in bed. Her game of nine-ball was certainly suffering, and she had to drop out of the league. But by now, she's more adjusted to the fast-track life, so as soon as she's free she joins her fellow nannies at the Irish Pub—or spends time with a Georgetown law student named Charles.

Janette and David barely remember what romance is these days. They have limited time for their active toddler, so, except for Spencer handoffs, they hardly even *see* each other.

But our nanny on Wilton Road has found true love.

12.

WHAT MAD DOGS, ENGLISHMEN, AND NANNIES SHOULD NEVER FORGET

O F COURSE WE WANT our nanny to enjoy her time off," my clients all say. *Their* lives may not be so balanced, but at least they recognize that a happy nanny is a better companion for their children. But the key word here is *balance*. No one wants to hire a party animal.

When checking a live-in nanny's references, I always ask former employers about her social life. How, and with whom, the newest member of your household spends her time off will affect the way she does her job. "We don't really care what she does after work," some clients say. Then after a pause I hear, *Just as long as it doesn't impact us.*

But when you're paying good money for your live-in nanny's daytime performance, you don't want her burning herself out at night or on weekends. Some nannies even have curfews, so unless they're lucky enough to have a separate entrance, live-in nannies often have to sneak in like dishonest teenagers. That could mean setting off the alarm system and waking the whole neighborhood—a considerable deterrent to a nanny's extracurricular activities.

Lucky nannies have a separate entrance to their quarters, an apartment over the garage, or even a cottage on the property. Apparently, such luxurious privacy can lead to other problems. An Alexandria family who lived on Mansion Drive housed their nanny from the Midwest in a pool house special enough to be featured in a *Washington Post* article about swanky nanny accommodations.

Years later, I ran into *that* nanny's former employer at my daughter's high school lacrosse game. As we watched our grown-up athletes race across the field, we reminisced about the days when our little girls still had nannies. "After we realized what was going on in that pool house, we fired her immediately," this former client said. "It was fine that our nanny was so *popular,* but who knew she was running a *brothel* on our property? Our neighbors didn't tell us a thing until she was gone. And then they couldn't wait to give us the graphic details."

The couple proceeded to tell me that pool house was full of exotic sex toys. Why is it that neighbors are only too willing to share what they know after the fact? I can't tell you how many times parents report that as soon as they let their nanny go, their neighbors suddenly had a lot of information to share. *She was always on her cell phone. I could hear her yelling at your child.* The mother has not only lost her nanny, but now she feels betrayed by her next-door neighbor.

If the *Post* had run a follow-up investigative report, we could have had our very own Washington scandal. Who knows who was visiting that pool house? As this lovely couple share these embarrassing details with me, I'm willing the lacrosse field to open up and swallow me into its depths.

Nannies with active social lives should live completely *out*. And even if your nanny says the only place she goes is *to church,* some faiths have such elaborate social calendars, this can mean she'll be busy every night of the week.

Most parents I work with can't remember what a social life actually *is.* They're on the Barney circuit: Gymboree, Mommy and Me, baby swim classes, Saturday T-ball with Daddy. If they get out at night, it's for a piano recital or a private-school fund-raiser, compulsory gala evenings that can cost as much as a cruise—because the couple ends up bidding on one.

So the nanny is having fun on her time off, and the resentful parents are doing laundry and paying bills on theirs. *How come she has a social life and we don't?* One couple purposely hired a sixty-year-old widow; they assumed she'd be beyond the dating stage and would remain with them for several years. Then their devoted, grandmotherly nanny unexpectedly fell in love and left her job to get married after six months.

Love means you never know when you're going to lose a nanny—or even a *manny.* Joe had a degree in Early Childhood Education but couldn't find a teaching job, so he decided to get some hands-on child-rearing experience working for a family with three boys. Their previous nanny had had so many car accidents that she was finally uninsurable, even though the father was an insurance executive.

Joe had a fine driving record, wrestling skills, and an excellent pitching arm, so he was the perfect person for the job. Then he walked into one of my nanny parties, and his eyes locked on to Jackie's. After the two were married, Jackie's employers let Joe move in with them—and they stayed for four years! Now the nanny and the manny have their own child, and while they've moved on to other careers, they're still very close to the families they used to work for.

My eight-year-old daughter is always the first to know when our nanny has a new boyfriend or has broken up with someone," one mother told me. "We're all totally involved in her love life." That was the mother who paid for her nanny's shrink sessions after her boyfriend left her for another nanny and she became depressed. (The list of nannies' perks seems to grow longer all the time.)

Another nanny turned her room into a shrine to her handsome policeman boyfriend. Her idea of an arts-and-crafts project with the children was making a collage of his photographs to hang in the family bathroom. When the mother took this masterpiece down, the nanny was incensed.

Most parents don't know what their nannies do during their off hours, until *he* appears on their doorstep. They may find out that their naïve nanny has given out their phone number and address to an untrustworthy stranger. And after the relationship breaks up, there might be a jilted ex-boyfriend stalker to deal with.

And the other extreme isn't much better: "Do you mind if James spends the night?"

Who is James? And, yes, we mind.

What comes to mind is the placement I tried to make for a Senate-subcommittee attorney who called me, *frantic*. The nanny she'd hired for her newborn decided not to show up, and she had to get back to work right away. Luckily, I had just heard about a candidate who lived right near Capitol Hill, a cheerful baby nanny anyone would love, with lots of experience.

"Bernice sounds wonderful," the euphoric attorney told me. "We're meeting tonight, and I'm sure I'll hire her." I felt like Superwoman, thrilled that I'd rescued another working damsel in distress.

When I heard Susan Jones's despondent message the next morning—"Call me. We need to talk"—I was really surprised.

"We *loved* Bernice. But we absolutely cannot hire her," Susan groaned. "Do you know about her boyfriend?"

"She mentioned she had one," I answered.

"Do you know where he *is*?"

Should I?

"He's in *jail!* " It got worse. The boyfriend wasn't just in jail—he was there for murder. Susan Jones had chatted with her nanny-to-be long enough to find out that through her church, Bernice did pastoral counseling with prisoners. That was how she had come to know—and love—the man who was serving a life sentence. One of my loveliest middle-aged nannies had betrothed herself to a convicted murderer. The boyfriend wasn't getting out any time soon, but my client wasn't taking any chances.

I eventually learned to ask nannies about their relationship history, even if they're divorced, ever since a Washington nanny's ex-husband showed up at her employer's home and actually *shot* her in front of the children. But our extensive credit, driving, and criminal-background checks on nannies don't reveal the same information about their lovers.

Back in Spring Valley, whenever Janette and David are actually there, they notice that their nanny's in a wonderful mood these days. But they're not.

Transactional attorneys like David at top D.C. firms are called "deal lawyers," junkies waiting for their next fix. Even though he's taken on the new hobby of paternity, he's still hot to trot. His specialty is helping American companies through the legal labyrinths of doing business abroad, so he commutes regularly to Asia and Africa. When he represented Kuwait, he was on twenty-four-hour call, but these days David only works his normal hundred-hour weeks—unless he's in Shanghai.

Janette, as we already know, is a media slave: Whatever White House news happens, whenever there's any "Presidential movement," she has to follow every minute of the story—even if her assignments are usually soft news: Bush's latest proclamation about the sanctity of the American family. Or how much he and Laura paid for income tax.

Thank goodness Emma remembered to write down when Spencer was due for booster shots. She even fixed the flat tire and got him to the pediatrician on time.

At least Janette is physically in town, because her husband hasn't spent more than a month at a time here in years. She's the multitasking mom (who delegates most of those tasks to Emma). David's more like a privileged frequent guest.

The tiring cliché about mothers doing a lot more of the day-to-day home and family work than dads isn't always true. But men don't usually notice details. When an Arlington couple called me recently, the dad described his children as "easy." According to him, the baby was on a great sleeping schedule and the two-year-old was "mellow."

Then his wife chimed in, unable to contain herself. "What are you talking about?" she shouted. "Our baby cries every night. You just don't hear her. You're the one who's on a great sleeping schedule."

Men do seem to go through life and parenting with different permission slips.

Another remote-control dad, a former ambassador, was helping his wife interview a prospective nanny. The mother asked the woman a lot of questions, but the father had only two: "Are you Catholic?" and "Are you a Democrat?" The nanny failed half of his exam, but they hired her anyway. And that was the last time he spoke to the nanny during the entire year she worked for him.

After losing another night's sleep because Spencer had an earache and screamed until she had to leave for Andrews Air Force base at three A.M., Janette decides to call David in Hong Kong to vent.

"What can I do from here?" he asks. Sensing her utter frustration, he sends her white roses: *To the best wife, mother, and journalist. Spencer and I love you.*

Definitely a nice gesture, but roses aren't enough. Janette and David need a vacation. A long weekend in the Caribbean isn't easy for either of them to pull off, but after her good work on her story about the President ordering Saddam Hussein to leave Iraq, Janette feels secure enough to request a Monday and a Friday off.

David hasn't gone anywhere not case-related in a few years, unless you count the ten hours he spent in the delivery room. He can only leave after his colleagues at the firm have taken their vacations during private-school spring break. Their families ski in Beaver Creek or windsurf on Maui. David will have to submit an absence memo so he can be phoned and/or BlackBerried at any billable moment. His clients expect total access in case they need emergency counsel.

Spencer and Emma are coming, too, by the way. So, going for broke, Janette rents interconnecting ocean-view rooms at Little Dix Bay on Virgin Gorda. *Because we're worth it.* And as soon as she does, the political climate in Spring Valley melts into a détente, according to Emma. Who's charged with buying everything Spencer needs for the trip, including a toddler just-like-Mommy toy laptop, and lots of waterproof #60 baby sunblock.

Books could be written about Taking Nanny on Vacation. The tales abound, many of them enviable. Young women from Whitefish, Montana, and Raymond, Maine, have stayed at the Plaza Athénée in Paris and the Savoy in London, just for starters. A nanny job can sound like a fabulous deal: your own vacation time off, as well as exotic trips with the family.

It can be. When a Virginia horse-country family needed a temporary nanny until they moved to Japan, we sent them Julia. They liked her so much they asked her to come work for them in Tokyo. Unbeknownst to us, Julia's lifelong dream had been to visit Japan, and she'd even studied the language. We chalked that one up to lucky nanny-placement karma.

Then there was the *National Geographic* photographer and his wife who were about to take their nanny to the Great Barrier Reef for a two-month project. A few days before they left, the (unmarried) nanny found out she was pregnant, so they needed someone to take her place, and even I was tempted. One of my former nannies, who'd become a teacher, had mentioned that she'd love a traveling nanny job over the summer.

When I asked, "Can you leave for Australia in forty-eight hours?" she started packing. And if she hadn't been stuck on the

Great Barrier Reef with the children from hell, or close to it, she'd have enjoyed the fantastic opportunity. Instead, she felt like one of those nineteenth-century British prisoners sent into forced labor Down Under: a nanny in exile. "I wouldn't have lasted more than a week if my employers hadn't blown eight thousand dollars on my last-minute ticket," she told me after she got home.

Even if you've worked for a family for years, round-the-clock vacation togetherness can be full of surprises. One of our star nannies accompanied two attorneys and their two children to Alaska, where they flew to an island to visit the polar bears. When the weather suddenly turned bad, there was only one six-seater seaplane to get them back to the mainland. "The nanny is utterly indispensable," this nanny mentioned, "until the plane can only take six people and *you're* number seven!"

Now we know what happened to the nannies on the *Titanic* after they ran out of lifeboats.

It's hard to resist another vacation-turned-disaster story. I'd already placed four highly educated nannies with a very discriminating family who summered in Jackson Hole, and they loved every one of them. Their newest nanny, Gina, was excited about the trip until she arrived a day early with the children and had to clean the enormous house, which was full of bugs and dead rodents.

Marooned in Wyoming, thousands of miles from her friends, Gina wasn't having the time of her life. "Don't you just love this job?" the family's glittery guests asked her at cocktail parties.

Feeling completely depressed, Gina cheered herself up by writing her twin sister a detailed letter about how she really felt about being on a working family vacation. She included "*South Park*–style" cartoons: Nanny taking a picture of the family on top of a mountain and encouraging them to back up until they fall off. Nanny cooking up poison pea soup for the children's lunch, etc.

If only Gina had mailed her letter instead of leaving it, unsealed, in the family jeep. After they opened it, the formerly completely sane parents were convinced they and their children were no longer safe with this nanny. They called the local sheriff and then they called me, referring to their summa cum laude graduate as "dumber than a box of rocks." The nanny "who'd made a death threat" was escorted off their property straight to the airport and put on the next flight home.

I have no idea why they faxed me the evidence the next day. The clients were shocked to find out how the nanny really felt about them. Those silly stick-figure drawings threatened only their egos—certainly not their lives! Despite my string of successes for them, they never called me again. You're only as good as your last placement.

B ut back to the vacation that promises to be utter nirvana for Janette and David. Spencer sleeps the whole way down (nothing like a little Benadryl), and when they finally land on Tortola and take a private launch to the remote resort, the vacation (for under $2,000 a day) promises to be a four-way honeymoon. Silvery blue water, tropical fruits and flowers, thatched huts for shade on the idyllic beach, cocktails brought to your chaise longue. Spencer has a blast with the deluxe set of sand toys Emma was smart enough to buy for him before they left.

Why didn't we do this sooner? Janette and David are actually reading *non-work-related* books. Her bureau chief knows where she is, but he's promised not to contact her unless he absolutely has to. And David only takes a few dozen phone calls a day, which is, in his world, absolutely nothing. Janette can live with it—as if she has a choice.

On the second ethereal Little Dix day, things are going so well that Janette tells her nanny to take the afternoon off. After slathering Spencer in #60, Emma disappears to dream on the sugar-white sand. When she wakes up, her fair British skin is a scary shade of pink.

The hotel doctor sends her to bed with ice packs and ointment. The next morning, Emma's still in too much pain to walk, let alone chase after Spencer or even lift him. Mom and Dad now get a real taste of what their nanny's eternal days with their son are like. While Emma sleeps, Janette and David can't seem to get their child to do anything they want him to. He runs them ragged starting at dawn, and won't even take a ten-minute nap. Spencer's normal routine is shot, and he has a sudden, bad case of the Terrible (almost) Twos: all speed and no judgment. He races down the beach daring to be caught, and almost runs into a waiter carrying a tray of drinks.

His nanny feels absolutely terrible, but it's clear she's out of commission for the rest of the vacation. Not the restful trip Janette had envisioned. After David finishes talking to a client in South Africa, he plays with Spencer in the water, making his son shriek with glee. Janette hardly ever sees how good he is with their child. Does David know that himself? Spencer's finally so tired from playing, he takes his first real nap since Emma's been off duty.

The romantic vacation turned out to be more of a *family* romance. Which is *not* what happened to another client, whose even more costly tropical getaway turned out to be a bad investment. A pharmaceutical-lobbyist client rented a $10,000 villa on St. Barts, hoping to revive her sex life and her failing marriage.

Her nanny was to share a room with their child and leave the parents in peace. Unfortunately, the bedrooms in that particular villa were next to each other, and the walls were Caribbean-thin, so the nanny was close enough to the action to feel like part of the marriage. When the mother suggested she sleep on the pull-out sofa in the living room, the nanny refused—until her employer threatened to send her home.

The vacation was a dismal failure anyway. The mother was stunned to discover in divorce court that her husband had been having an affair with their plain-Jane nanny. Robin Williams and his nanny aside, I can assure you that after twenty years in this business, very few dads date their nannies.

My clients must all be too *busy*.

13.

THE
WASHINGTON ZOO

ONCE THE HUNTINGTON-WILDERS are home from what turned out to be the vacation with a silver lining, their still-tender nanny wants to see her boyfriend. After Emma's ordeal on Virgin Gorda, Janette can hardly refuse her a quick visit from Charles—after she puts Spencer to bed, since she and David have to switch themselves back into super-high work gear.

Unfortunately, a neighbor has a different attitude about Charles. He was supposed to arrive around nine, right after his night class, but he stopped at the law library. By the time he pulls up in his ten-year-old Honda Civic (a red flag on Wilton Road) and approaches Emma's lower-level entrance, it's almost eleven.

Unfortunate timing. Next door, heating up some cocoa, the retired government official *with the best of intentions* spots what can only be an intruder: a black male walking through the yard at midnight. Following protocol, he immediately calls 911. By the time he finds Janette and David's number to alert them about the stranger entering their home, the squad cars are on their way.

Bright lights and deafening sirens make this a great reunion for Emma and Charles. Thank God for the Spring Valley Neighborhood Watch.

On this occasion, Janette is all for censorship of the local evening news.

After everyone on Wilton Road recuperates from the embarrassing mixup, Charles is ready to escape the scene of the "crime." Emma needs all the sleep she can get, since her employers will both disappear in a few hours and leave her to help Spencer readjust to normal.

David unpacks and packs again for ten days in Tokyo and Singapore. Janette has to be ready when the President welcomes home two liberated prisoners of war who served in Iraq, and the following day she'll cover the First Lady's annual Easter Egg Roll on the South Lawn.

Once she and David got used to spending so much time with Spencer and learned his routine—and he got used to having *them* around, it was a love-fest. Ironically, if their nanny hadn't been out of commission, these wistful parents wouldn't have discovered how wonderful it was to be a self-sufficient threesome, with their child.

Lazy, fun island life is *over*. But David has a terrific surprise in the works for his wife and son. Given his and Janette's impossible schedules, their son may have to remain an only child. But what if Spencer had a four-footed "sibling" to grow up with? Janette still talks about her childhood golden retriever, Lucky. So, between his Pacific Rim meetings and late-night conference calls, David's been researching kennels.

But even though Emma doesn't count in these demographics, she's the one who'll have to house-train the puppy—while trying to teach Spencer the same skill set. It's a good thing David was smart enough to discuss this big decision with *her* before he ordered the puppy—female—to even out the sexes in the family.

I spend so much time dealing with people's animals that it sometimes feels like I'm running a veterinary service. Whether the nanny or the family has a pet (or six), animal issues always make my job more challenging than it already is.

By nature, nannies are warm, caring individuals with strong maternal instincts who love children and animals. Watch a newly arrived, red-blooded American girl unpack her suitcase, and lurking somewhere inside will be a teddy bear or an entire stuffed menagerie, as well as framed pictures of her former pets.

Then there are the nannies' *live* creatures.

"Hi, Kimberly, this is Barbara from White House Nannies. We were so excited to receive your application." *No kidding.* She sounds like an authentic, purebred midwesterner. So few of them still want to be nannies I'd be the first to advocate cloning if it would increase our pool of great applicants. Back in Wisconsin, Kimberly's just another twenty-year-old looking for a job, but in the Washington childcare market, she's a hot commodity.

She sounds great: seven years of experience, some college, and her references say she walks on water. She takes initiative, has great judgment, and children love her. She plays piano *and* soccer, and she weighs in at under 200 pounds. I'm salivating. Five families will kill for Kimberly.

"Really? Well, I'm excited, too. I can't wait to move to D.C."

I ask the standard questions to figure out which of our families will be best for Kimberly until she interrupts me to ask, "How will they feel about my ferrets?" Elvis and Madonna are adorable, and they're coming with her.

Thank God Kimberly can't see my face. "This may make it a tad harder to find the right family for you, but I'll see what we can do." My perfect placement is totally unplaceable, at least until I research the relative toxicity of the ferret species. What diseases do they carry? Do they bite? Maybe tomorrow's mail will yield hotter prospects, but as of today, this ferret fanatic is *stone cold*.

Other nannies come with more benign critters: tropical fish, gerbils, rabbits. Birds are usually okay, not counting special circumstances, such as were in effect when a judge's wife called me for advice.

"Everything *was* fine with the new nanny," Virginia Weatherall says despairingly. "But I don't know how to handle what happened over the weekend." Virginia is a genuinely nice, smart woman who lives in your standard WASP Colonial. The interior is *greige,* nothing loud or aggressive such as *color.* She wears jewel-neck sweaters, skirts below the knee, sensible black pumps, one strand of pearls, and a tasteful short coiffure: the Washington bureaucratic uniform.

Virginia and her husband have two very active children, so I'm afraid the nanny has had a problem with them—but I'm wrong. "Jeremy went down to the basement to check the fuse box. Cara had left her door slightly ajar when she went away for the weekend. We would never, *ever* go into her room without her permission, but my husband smelled a noxious odor coming from her room, so he felt compelled to peek in. Then he spotted Cara's bird. Dead. I mean really dead. Are we allowed to say anything? We don't want to offend Cara, and we know it's her private space . . ."

Did I ever complain that my job gets old—because a dead bird is a new one for me. I tell Virginia, "Try *I'm really sorry your bird died. But do you think you could get it out of your room sometime soon?* Maybe you could help Cara arrange a small funeral service." (Where do I come up with these ideas? I'm glad she didn't ask me to suggest appropriate music.)

"The judge really believes in the right to privacy, and he doesn't want to be accused of breaking and entering. But after all, this is our house." She's married to the judge but she's asking *me* about their rights?

American-born nannies usually adore pets, but many of our foreign nannies consider animals, well . . . animals. That belong outside. They're horrified that Fifi sleeps on the parents' bed, eats the same food they do, and gets as much attention as the children. I asked a nanny from Ethiopia if she'd work in a home where there was a dog. "I'll take the job," she said, "as long as I don't have to talk to the dog as if he's a human." "I definitely understand how you feel," I told her. Then as soon as I got off the phone I started talking to my miniature schnauzer Wally as if he were my favorite child—which my children swear he is.

Here's an actual excerpt from a recent client's application:

"My firstborn twins are my beloved King Charles cavalier spaniels, love-bunny lapdogs. But they're still a little *puzzled* by our one-year-old, and I feel constantly guilty about not spending enough time with them. Walking the dogs and the baby simultaneously is way too difficult. So I'm looking for someone to bond with the new baby while I make sure the doggies don't get jealous. We plan to ask our dog trainer to come out and work with the nanny to make sure she understands their needs."

Excuse me? Instead of farming out the dogs, she wants to farm out the *baby*? I scribble *Suggest Doggie Day Care* on that application, while thinking unkind thoughts about this client.

So *family* pets are deal breakers, too. Take the Bernsteins, who've been clients forever. Each year we call to update their files: "Okay, let's see here. Samantha is now ten and Jonathan is seven. Do you still have the snakes, the dog, the cats, and the hamster?" I say a silent, fervent prayer that Mrs. Bernstein will tell me they no longer have the anaconda.

"Well, actually, there are a few changes this year. We got a chinchilla, a hedgehog, and of course, we still have Eleanor and Rigby. The snakes. Sad to say, the cats and the hamster are no longer with us."

Their former nannies still have nightmares from watching the kids feed the snakes their daily live mouse rations. Maybe we should be looking for a temp zookeeper for the Bernsteins instead of a nanny.

Then I hear from Lydia Hayes of Alexandria. Long legs, tan in the middle of the winter, frosted hair, clipped voice, not warm and fuzzy. "Trevor and Brinkly are on a great schedule now. I'm out during the day doing volunteer work, so I need someone energetic and outdoorsy to get them to the park in the morning and back home for a nap. Nanny will give them lunch before getting them outside again for more exercise . . ."

"How old are your children, Mrs. Hayes?"

"My children? My children are now seventeen and twenty-one. One's at Andover and the other's finishing at Williams. The nanny is for our Portuguese water dogs."

Sounds like another job for Bone Jour puppy kindergarten. But at least Lydia spent time with her human children, too, when they were around.

Cats are the bane of a nanny agency's existence, the death knell for many, many placements.

"So, I see on your application that you have three Persian cats."

"Yes, we're a blended family. My husband had two when we married and I had one. They get along beautifully." Unfortunately, for every cat owner there are ten phobic or deathly-allergic-to-felines nannies. And since cats live from ten to twenty years, by the time I can find this couple a cat-crazy nanny, their children will be old enough to take care of themselves.

After my wonderful nanny Marta left us, she was hired to take care of a newborn for a three-cat family. Marta's file stated clearly that she disliked cats, but the parents fell in love with her and offered her the job, promising her that the cats wouldn't go near her bedroom. But either they lied, or their cats did. Her second night on the job, Marta woke up screaming with all three cats perched on her head. And when she quit, the family was angry with *me*. Go figure.

Call it obsessive-compulsive behavior. Otherwise, why would I willingly opt to pick up the phone at five-fifteen on a Friday afternoon? Maybe the perfect nanny or the perfect job is on the other end of that line.

The conversation starts out with real promise: She's a doctor with a baby, and they live in Rockville, Maryland, a good location for our nannies. But that was the end of the good stuff, and as the call progressed, my eyes started rolling in my head.

"Four large dogs and three cats? And you'll be working at home for the foreseeable future?" I don't get it—a doctor working at home, and the real emphasis is on the pets?

I can't resist, "So, are you a vet?"

"No. We just love animals, and it's very important that the nanny love them, too."

"We" are she and her female companion. So, what we have is four large dogs, three cats, and a lesbian couple working from home. Oh, and a baby. Filling this job won't be easy, but I'll try.

Hey, wait a minute. What about Kimberly and her adorable ferrets? Maybe I have a match made in (animal) heaven!

Luckily, like many of her British compatriots, Emma is a true dog lover, and she's already housebroken several of her own pets, so she's up for the extra responsibility. "Spencer will adore a pet," she assures David. And since Emma's due for a raise anyway, he'll have to take her new canine responsibilities into account.

If animals break a lot of deals, parsimonious clients break even more of them. I absolutely understand when couples truly can't afford to pay their nanny more than twelve dollars an hour. We work hard to help clients economize in many ways to pay for great childcare, and we don't push anyone to pay more than they can. I understand how expensive this kind of care is, and I'm not even sure at this point I could afford my own service.

But I have a hard time dealing with clients who obviously have the money to pay a nanny what she's worth, but find it difficult to do so. *How much do I have to pay her?* You'd think their nanny wasn't entitled to earn a living taking care of their children, that she should love them enough to take care of them for free.

But there are attorneys who bill at three to four hundred dollars an hour who actually think in terms of giving their nannies 50¢-an-hour raises after they've performed wonderfully for months. *My neighbor pays her nanny four hundred a week and she cleans the house and does the laundry and the cooking.* Whenever I hear about a great bargain down the street, my eyes roll and I start to multi-task to make up for the time I'm now wasting.

"If someone is willing to take eight dollars an hour, are you sure you want that person to take care of your child?" I've asked too many times.

There's often a strange disconnect. Parents expect the world of their nannies but don't want to pay her for those qualities. If I tell clients the going rate is between $12 and $15 an hour and, judging from their professions, they can easily pay that, the answer is often, "We're thinking of starting her at eleven. *We want to have someplace to go.*"

The double-partner couple in my neighborhood comes to mind—the ones who live in a $1.5-million house with two—or is it three?—Mercedes parked in front. Their firm's salary ranges were recently published in the *Washingtonian,* by the way, so I'm not speculating about their ability to pay the household help a living wage.

This is the client who expects me to hand-deliver her fifteen (count 'em) nanny applications, and who reviewed just as many applications from my colleague at Nanny Nation.

No one was quite right. Not one of these women matched the profile the ultra-entitled woman felt would "play well" in Shepherd Park. Her neighbor had a Filipina nanny and she needed a Filipina as well so the nannies would be friends. And even after this client hired a nanny from Nancy, she kept calling me to make sure she wasn't missing out on anyone "great."

More obscenities rush through my mind and almost out my mouth. I've spent hours on this non-placement, and she's still calling just to make sure she got the best possible deal after all.

Another of my least-favorite stories proves, yet again, that there's no such thing as a free lunch. As in: that lovely lunch Alexa Trudeau treated me to at Charlie Palmer's so we could get to know each other. Just as I'd done for her father-in-law, I found Alexa a wonderful nanny, a Buddhist live-out from Nepal who worked for the Trudeaus for several months without any problems.

Another rule of the game: If I've always dealt with the mother, and the *father* is suddenly on the line, *be prepared*. So I'm not thrilled to hear Alan's booming, businesslike, "*Hello, Barbara.*" He's had nothing to do with the nanny arrangements, and Alexa has been very happy with Mira. Why is this total non-player suddenly complaining about the young woman as if she's brought the plague into his home?

"What exactly is she doing wrong?" I ask, trying to remain civilized even though *he* certainly isn't.

"I don't know where to begin," he spits at me arrogantly. "She doesn't even know how to make *cinnamon toast.*"

"Gee," I say, stifling a laugh, "I don't think they eat cinnamon toast in Nepal." The rest of his complaints are equally absurd. The real issue is that Alan and Alexa's two boys are out of control, and since *they're* not willing to whip those boys into shape, they expect their gentle Buddhist nanny to do it.

I let Alan rant until I hear his memorable best line:

"You know, Barbara, if I'm not happy with a watch from Cartier, they take it back and give me a new one."

Did he just say that to me? Does real-estate big-shot Trudeau really think he's *bought* his nanny and that he can *return* her, as if she's a *commodity*?

I'm livid. That's the end of the Trudeaus, no matter where they want to take me for lunch.

14.

WHO'S BEEN SLEEPING IN MY BED?

I'M ALWAYS HAPPY to hear from Emma, whose calls are like sunshine. She's still grateful for her current job, especially since her former employers treated her so miserably. Their seven-bedroom McLean home was so filthy after their weekend parties, Emma couldn't *function* until she spent all her free time cleaning it while the children were in preschool. The children were so *monstrous,* trying to control them was even harder than all that cleaning she wasn't paid to do.

This job, Emma has assured me, is *"easy peasy."*

At least it *used* to be. Today I hear some actual angst in her voice. Janette has been working more than "occasional" nights and weekends lately, something to do with a ratings war and her heartless executive producer. But at least she *sees* her child, sometimes even when he's awake.

The last time David called from Singapore, Emma heard Janette tell him, "Get home soon or your son won't recognize you."

David is supposed to do the weekly supermarket runs, but the nanny ends up with all his leftover errands and chores. No one ever calls Emma a house manager, but she is. She's also Spencer's potty coach. He likes watching his *Potty Time* DVD, but he isn't making progress, and the process involves frequent accidents. Emma definitely earns her keep.

Everyone's thrilled when Ginger the golden retriever arrives. Emma's excited, too, until she realizes she's stuck cleaning up the puppy messes. The non-human member of the family has to be housebroken, exercised, taken to the groomer and to the vet for shots. When Emma isn't reading about how to toilet-train Spencer, she's studying the puppy manuals, but there's no progress on either front.

Emma is almost ready to join the Overworked Nannies Club. The Turtle Park members commiserate, advise one another, and cheer themselves up about absentee or divorcing parents, over-scheduled, underdisciplined children, and their pets. Nannies almost always get more than they bargain for: full sinks and dishwashers, laundry the parents "did" but left in the dryer to be folded and put away, overflowing Diaper Genies and trash bins, filthy kitchen floors, and, worst of all, no food in the house—and no money to buy any.

Emma still feels lucky when she hears her friends' complaints. But now that she's worked on Wilton Road for almost a year, she needs something to keep her going. "I want to stay," she tells me. "But I need more money." Like every other nanny I've ever placed, Emma circled her first-year anniversary on the calendar as soon as she took the job.

Seven hundred and fifty dollars a week is still a very good live-in salary, but by now Emma puts in many more hours than she signed up for. Unless her employers do something, she's ready to move on.

"How much are you thinking about?" I ask Emma. Money can be an uncomfortable topic for nannies and clients alike. I don't ever suggest how much anyone should earn or pay, but I try to help them figure it out.

When a situation has to be renegotiated, a nanny and her employer often call me the same day. When Janette calls from work, I'm not surprised. She knew she was expecting too much of her nanny, even before she picked up Emma's discontented vibes. Janette's fear of losing face time at the network is only surpassed by the even more ominous fear she'll lose her nanny.

She does not want to go through life without Emma.

"What should I do to keep her happy?" Janette asks me. I'd much rather hear this question than: *How much would I have to pay a new nanny?* Parents who think they'll save money by changing nannies figure out quickly that, besides the trouble of interviewing and adjusting to a new nanny, they'd end up paying her more as well as giving me another commission. Clients pay me a one-time fee of 12 percent of a nanny's yearly salary, and 15 percent for a live-in nanny.

It's almost always better to give their current nanny a raise. But no formula or guidebook can tell you what your nanny's worth. Clients usually increase salaries by a certain percentage every year, often the standard cost-of-living increase. Some promise their nannies a raise when *they* get one, which was a better idea during the boom years of the '90s than it is today.

Clients come up with a variety of interesting ways to reward their nannies for jobs well done. "We need to give her a raise,"

WHO'S BEEN SLEEPING IN MY BED?

I've heard, "but can you help us be *creative*?" In other words, *We don't want to part with any more actual money and put those extra taxable dollars on the books.*

"We take our nanny with us twice a year to Hawaii, so we'll give her some time off during those trips."

"She can stay with the children in our villa in Tuscany. I'm sure she'll be grateful for such a fabulous opportunity."

As if caring for their children in a glamorous location will increase the nanny's value on the open market when she's ready for her next job. No matter how you finagle it, nannies, not to mention Internal Revenue, expect actual increases in cold, hard cash. *Not* a new stereo system, even though it's worth fifteen hundred dollars, and *not* a week in the family's cabin in Maine—even without the family.

God help the employers who don't pay attention to their nanny at this critical juncture. Unethical agencies call the nannies they've placed when their years are up, hoping to entice them into taking new jobs so they can earn second placement fees for the same nannies.

Washington nanny-napping tales abound in which great women are lured from good positions by irresistibly higher salaries. A physician mother who'd been negligent about paying her hardworking nanny what she was worth came home in time to see the young woman driving away in a U-Haul.

I'm relieved that Janette's safely on board. "Everyone likes to know they're appreciated," I tell her. I'll work on her behalf as well as her nanny's without betraying confidences. "What would make Emma smile—time, money—or a combination of the two?" I ask. Everyone has different priorities, so parents need to offer their nanny a "package" she'll feel good about accepting.

I advise clients to pay their nannies the "market" rate; an underpaid nanny will soon find out she should be earning more. Medical and dental insurance are often added to salaries. Representative Bill Paxon and his wife, Representative Susan Molinari, generously gave their nannies extra money every month for their health insurance. But after one of them had a serious car accident and the Congressman called the ambulance, the nanny refused to go to the hospital. "This is why we got you insurance," he argued. Unbeknownst to my clients, the nanny had cancelled the policy they had been underwriting and have given her boyfriend the health insurance money.

Why should I pay her to watch TV? I hear this all the time, and it's code for "taking a break." As if a nanny who cares for a demanding infant all day long doesn't have the right to some downtime while the baby is sleeping.

Clients also give their nannies health-club memberships, year-end bonuses, and retirement plans. I've even heard about parents who reward their nannies when their child reaches a developmental milestone. "She taught our baby to talk *months* before his friends, so we gave her a spa weekend," one mother mentioned. A dermatologist's nanny got facials and lip waxes as her "signing bonus."

Some highly educated Washington parents are happy to pay their nannies' college tuition. A high-tech mother even agreed to come home early two nights a week so her nanny could take education classes. After a few years, she started to wonder when the nanny was going to graduate. And it was odd that she never mentioned her courses or brought home any books.

Even stranger, when the nanny left for her classes, she wasn't exactly dressed like a college student. They decided to hire a private investigator, who discovered that the nanny spent her evenings at a cowboy bar in suburban Virginia. She was studying a profession they don't usually teach at community colleges.

Nannies originally hired to take care of school-age children sometimes have less to do once the children are more independent. Instead of getting raises, these caregivers continue at their now-easier job at the same rate of pay; one woman actually worked for *ten years* without a raise.

I don't advocate this kind of arrangement: Who works for a decade without making more money? The children were home less of the time, but the parents were unavailable, so they needed someone on call when their children were ill and during vacations and snowstorms. (Washington schools are famous for shutting down if there's a "blizzard"—often only a dusting—even if the streets are perfectly clear.)

"You're paying for *continuity* in your household," I tell clients, which is always a worthwhile investment. If more independent children leave nannies with free time, there are always errands to run, laundry to do, appointments and play dates to book.

No one likes change. When contracts are renegotiated, job descriptions evolve along with salaries. One mother decided she wanted her nanny to start polishing the silver. "She's only supposed to do domestic chores related to the *children*," I reminded her.

"I know," she said. "It is the children's silver!" This was a rare moment when I had no idea what to say!

A cable-news producer used to tell me she loved her nanny because "Who else could I send to Lord and Taylor's to buy my bras?" (As far as I know, no one else has put that job on their nanny's To Do list.)

On benches in local parks from Friendship Heights to Northwest D.C. to Reston, Virginia, the same conversation is taking place: *How much do they pay you?* Some nannies feel fine about their jobs until their peers tell them they're not being paid enough. But the "union" can be wrong: A young nanny who was encouraged to leave a cushy job found out she was still too inexperienced to make what her friends told her she was worth.

Caregivers who think they're overworked and undercompensated often find out that other nannies work longer hours for less money. And then there's the nanny in the park with a Cheshire-cat smug smile who knows she has the best deal in town.

But she's not talking.

Janette and Emma soon agree on their new contract: eight hundred dollars a week, three weeks of paid vacation, as well as the expected Christmas bonus. In addition, Emma can start ordering the groceries from Peapod instead of dragging Spencer to the supermarket. And best of all, Janette will hire a puppy trainer—until Ginger's housebroken.

Now I can get back to some of my other "only" clients. I try to make each of them feel I'm that devoted to *their* childcare needs.

2:30

Media executive mom-with-blended-family calls. *He* has a teenager, *she* has a teenager, and *they* have two toddlers. I've known her for years: Her second husband isn't home to help any more than her first one was.

It seems that the au pair this publishing executive hired from France—without my help, by the way—has been joining the sixteen-year-old boy in bed. I'd have put her on the next plane to Paris. But the young woman is great at handling the extremely difficult toddlers, so apparently the mother's willing to overlook those "indiscretions." Much to my *horror*, instead of requesting a new nanny, she wants me to find her "another set of hands to keep things running smoothly."

In my opinion, there are too many hands in that household as it is.

But at least the son will do well on his French Achievement exam.

3:00

A congressman's wife wants to know how my agency works—in great detail. *What if we hire a nanny and then decide we don't need her after all? . . . Do we really have to eat with her?* etc. As soon as she hears "twelve percent of the nanny's first-year salary and fifteen percent if she lives in," there's silence for a long time. Until I hear, "Well, *that's* a lot of money."

3:45

Client in Chevy Chase offers a Guatemalan woman $650 a week to live in. She has twenty years of experience, has worked with large families, and is even a gourmet chef, but she has no formal education. The same client was willing to pay seven hundred dollars a week to a college grad from Tennessee who's just starting out. The Latin-American woman, who's worth much more, supports her entire family back home on her salary. For many of my clients, American college grads represent the gold standard.

Priorities, priorities.

4:45

A twenty-two-year-old nanny from small-town Missouri, who's obviously not tuned in to current events, calls next.

She's reluctant to take the great job she's been offered because it involves five "floating hours" for possible work emergencies. The parents have assured her they won't just call at the last minute to say they'll be five hours late. "The mom works for Homeland Security," I explain, "so her life might be a little unpredictable."

After a dead silence I hear, "Is Homeland Security some kind of a home mortgage company?"

5:00

The next nanny who calls has already quit her job—for a good reason. Her employer works from five-thirty P.M. until two A.M., not the eight-to-six schedule she signed on for. She got this job, by the way, through an online nanny service, so you get what you pay for. This young woman, from the Kentucky Bible Belt, does not belong with a mother who earns her cash at the downtown strip joint called Camelot.

It'll be easy to find her another job. I just hope the stripper mom doesn't call me looking for a new nanny.

5:12

Some days seem to have themes. "My nanny has been taking naps in our bed with the baby," the next caller says. "Now the baby won't fall asleep in her crib." Let's call this the Goldilocks syndrome.

Five minutes later, I hear from a mom who found out her nanny was "sleeping on the job" while the baby was napping. This presents a dilemma for me, too. I understand why the mother's annoyed. But the nanny works eleven-hour days, starting at seven, after an hour's commute, and leaves after dinner, so of course she needs some down-time.

I try to explain this, but the mother isn't listening.

I'm ready for a nap myself, but I still need to look at my mail. The first envelope I open contains a large *floor plan* of a rather impressive home in Maryland horse country. Is this for real? Are they trying to sell me their house, or are they looking for a nanny? There are several envelopes with our favorite kind of mail: signed waivers and accompanying checks for our services. But sometimes I end up rummaging through the wastebasket.

The nicest letter of the day is from a mother who's thanking us for finding her the nanny she's had for the past four years:

I just learned that Jeremy scored in the 100th percentile in second-grade reading, and in the upper 90th percentile in mathematics. He also did well on the Raven test. Whatever that is. We could never have done any of this without the fine and gracious help of White House Nannies.

I wasn't expecting this, but it's nice to know.

Have I mentioned the calls from nannies looking for work? Since we're the United Nations, we hear so many interesting accents around here, including some pretty foreign-sounding American ones. I'm not expecting perfect language skills and I try hard to put the caller at ease. But as soon as I hear "You have job for me? How much you pay?" I brace myself for another version of *Lost in*

Translation. "Tell me about your childcare experience," I ask. If the response is dead air—or worse, a non sequitur: "Tell me your name" and the response is "One baby"— the call is going to be brief. Believe me, given Washington's nanny shortage, I try hard not to eliminate any great foreign candidates, but good communication is an important part of the job.

5:38

I have to answer a hundred questions during the call I'm sorry I take from an over-thorough new dad who's a corporate attorney. He finally asks the perennial favorite new-client question: "So, Barbara. What percentage of your placements don't work out?"

"We don't keep those figures." I have to bite my tongue, but he's relentless.

My husband tells me what I should have said to this client: *I'll be happy to tell you that information. After you tell me what percentage of legal cases you lose.*

I wish I'd thought of that myself.

5:59

It seems like my day will really end on a high note when I hear from a lovely Potomac mother who wants a nanny for her first baby so she can get back to work. She's just decorated the nursery and the nanny suite, and she's willing to pay top dollar.

I put her application in an envelope immediately, asking, "Do you have any special requests?"

"No," she says sweetly. "Just don't send us any *schvartzes.*"

That envelope goes straight into the trash.

We start out every day in Charming Mode, but it's not easy to be civil by the end.

I'm outta here.

15.

MORE INFORMATION
THAN I NEEDED—OR
NOT ENOUGH

WHEN YOU'RE IN the childcare business, you find out a lot more about some families than you ever expected to: odd eating and sleeping habits, unusual ideas about discipline, surprising priorities. I hear it all, and to tell you the truth, I'd rather not know.

Okay, I'm lying. Just when I think I'm having a ho-hum day, an intriguing scenario revives my interest in my work. "We just can't decide which nanny to hire," sighs the entrepreneur from Alexandria. Lillian is older, a great long-term candidate, lots of experience and references, and the real bonus is she's a fabulous cook. Jessica's a recent college grad, adorable and competent, but she only wants to work for a year until she starts grad school. Her idea of cuisine is microwavable mac-and-cheese.

Both nannies want the same salary. It's a no-brainer.

But I hope Lillian hasn't started packing yet, because the couple change their minds right after they hire her.

This mother of three young children whispers, "Let me close my door," a common refrain in my business. Employees aren't supposed to have, or at least think about, their children during working hours. "I guess it boils down to sex," she giggles. That's one way to get my undivided attention, and as a professional, I certainly need the rest of the story.

"Well, the kids still sleep in our bed. I know, I know, we've *got* to get them out—so Ed and I make love in the other rooms of the house."

I'm still wondering what this family-bed business has to do with hiring the nanny who can only stay for a year. By the time they get used to her, they'll have to go through the interviewing and breaking-in process all over again. They must have a pretty good reason to put themselves through all that.

"Let me explain," she says. "We found out that Jessica visits her boyfriend on the weekends. We love Lillian, but she'd be here *all* the time. My husband says if we hire her, we'll never have sex again."

Who could argue with that decision?

I write "nanny should go *away* on weekends" on their file, for next year.

There goes my theory that New-Agey Marylanders have family beds and old-fashioned Virginians keep their children locked out of the master bedroom.

We send prospective clients a two-page application, but some clients need a lot more space to fully answer our questions. We often get back a long document informing us about the parents' taste in music and art, where they've traveled, and how they get their exercise. And if, by chance, any family member has gone to Harvard or Princeton, if we haven't read about it, they'll find some excuse to slip that information into our conversation.

All the Ivies have cachet in this town, but those two groups are proudest of their pedigrees.

When I hear, for instance, *I'm very active in my college alumni group,* I fall right into the trap of asking a parent, "Oh. Where did you go to school?"

By the way: I, too, went to Harvard—summer school, that is, where I took Picaresque Literature, a course that has served me *so well* in my professional life.

But my clients' innumerable degrees are only the beginning. No data is too insignificant for them to mention: every place they've ever lived, their love for mountains and lakes, their professions—and their parents'—in detail, including the fact that they enjoy "spirited political discussions over a good bottle of wine."

I spent my junior college year in Finland and another year in Italy, and I speak a passable German. My husband is fluent in Russian as well as the Native American language of Crow. I love Ohio State football and he loves Wake Forest basketball and all forms of auto racing, especially Formula 1.

I guess I should be on the lookout for a hoop-shooting, Finnish-speaking nanny who won't mind watching the children when she isn't racing sports cars.

Did I forget to mention the children's schedules we receive? Just in case a child isn't getting enough from her private school, or her public school's Gifted and Talented program, parents often make sure I know he or she spends every waking moment productively. An eight-year-old girl's Spring Schedule is on my desk right now:

MONDAY: swimming 6:30–7:30
TUESDAY: French 3:25–4, gymnastics 5–8
WEDNESDAY: drums 6–6:30, catechism 7–8 P.M.
THURSDAY: French 3:15–4, gymnastics 4:30–8
FRIDAY: swimming 5:30–6:30
SUNDAY: religious school 10–12, drama 2–3:30

Good news about Saturday, though; it's Family Day: no formally scheduled activities.

A certain insurance CEO never forgets to update me about his two-year-old prodigy who's fluent in three languages and can tell one Beethoven symphony from another. *Yes,* I say at least once a day, All *my clients tell me their children are brilliant. But yours is off the charts.*

What will all these exceptional children be like when they grow up?

Even though this proud dad's wife doesn't seem to work outside—or *inside*—the home, he's always the one who calls. He thinks their energetic child is tiring out his delicate trophy wife, leaving her no energy to play with him. He goes on to explain how hard it is to lure her into bed and some of his strategies.

I'm sparing you the details (even though he didn't spare me), but we finally get around to their childcare needs. I try to rescue *this* couple's sex life by sending them three lively nannies. None of them gets hired. Maybe this mother has already decided who she'd rather have fun with.

I don't have time for idle speculations. Time to move on to the client with extrasensory perception.

"My husband used to date strippers," an attorney informs me after a twenty-minute interview with a lovely Filipina nanny. "If he says she was flirting with him, he knows what he's talking about," she says adamantly. I haven't been to a strip joint lately, but that nanny is definitely not the type who works in one, so it's hard to hide my skepticism.

"Are you sure that's what was going on?" I inquire gently.

"Absolutely," the mother insists. "He picked up her subliminal messages *loud and clear.*" These clients have already interviewed a dozen nannies, and that's just from *my* agency. It's nice to get input from both spouses, but this feedback is so out-there, I'm starting to get the picture: This placement might not happen. (P.S. It didn't.)

And then there are the cases in which my clients have too much information. The mother who prosecutes child abusers for the Crimes Against Children department of the FBI knew all sorts of things I'd never want to know. She hears about so many gruesome cases that when it came to hiring a nanny, she was terrified. If I knew what *she* knew, I'd have a hard time trusting someone with my child, too.

Nannies are overloaded with unnecessary data, too. When they don't know what to do with what they know, they tell us all about it. "She keeps inviting me to have tea with her in the kitchen," a sweet nanny from Georgia explained. "She told me she never should have married her husband and that she ruined her life. I know she just needs someone to talk to, but she's only paying me to take care of the children. I think she needs a shrink."

Another nanny needing to talk was taking care of a ten-year-old boy who swore a blue streak at her and dumped her pocketbook upside down. When his colorful vocabulary failed him, he *spit.* The child's mother said Timothy was just "going through a phase." The last straw was when the mother sent her nanny to

Timmy's anger-management therapist. The therapist told the nanny, "Just be an adult and deal with it."

Who licensed *him*?

The nanny quit the job. As soon as the mother realized she was now the victim of Timothy's angry "phase," she called me for help. I was fresh out of masochistic nannies that week.

"They're getting a divorce" I hear from a hardworking nanny in Georgetown. "Now I'll have to take care of the children in his house *and* in her house." Do I also need to know this father broke up with his wife and his girlfriend at the same time? And that the girlfriend was their *marriage counselor*?

Who picked *her*?

Another nanny tells me about the unfortunate Friday night when her employer invited his staff over for a "meeting." His environmental-attorney wife was away at a conference. "I went out on a date that night, but I had a terrible time so I came home early," the nanny explains. Her boss's miniskirted secretary opened the door, not exactly thrilled to see her.

"Why don't you take a nice long ride?" the boss said, throwing her the keys to his Porsche—the car he never let his wife drive. She drove around until she almost ran out of gas, but the "meeting" was still going on when she crept back to her room at two A.M.

My colleague Nancy at Nanny Nation graciously referred clients in Bethesda to me. (That should have been a red flag. Why didn't she want them?) Their ex-nanny had already called me for a new job. Not only were her former employers nudists, but she walked into the baby's nursery one day and found them on the floor making love.

Who could make this up?

But many parents who easily share salacious details about their sex lives are less eager to reveal what I really *do* need to know. As if the nanny won't have to deal with their child's eating disorder, or with a learning-disabled sixth-grader with hours of homework.

Everyone is aware of the large spectrum of children's issues, which seems to be increasing. I understand parents' discomfort. I've dealt with a few of these challenges myself and can certainly empathize. But whether it's a colicky baby with reflux, a preschooler diagnosed with ADHD, or a child with oppositional behavior disorder, full disclosure helps us find the right nanny for each special situation.

Unfortunately, super-accomplished parents often have a hard time accepting "failings" in their children. I listen carefully for subtle hints: "My child is very bright, but she can be a little inappropriate." "My child has high energy," a corporate mother mentions. "By the way"—she lowers her voice—"*this is not code for ADHD.*"

Besides coping with these children for many more hours each week than their parents do, the nanny has to take them from one appointment to the next, and sometimes they're kicking and screaming: occupational, speech, and physical therapists; psychologists and tutors of every stripe. The good news about these interventions is that the family's getting help. But the bad news is, guess who has to do all the follow-through?

Once I understand the situation, I can identify a nanny with the right experience and attitude to care for these children. Whether it's PDD, sensory integration disorder, Asperger's or Williams Syndrome, a compassionate nanny can make a huge difference in these children's and their parents' lives.

. . .

I'm as much of a newsaholic as the next Washingtonian, so I don't miss the truly exciting stories Janette has been covering this week. Thanks to the press gaggle aboard Air Force One en route to Louisville, her exciting agenda includes meeting a member of the Freedom Corps, visiting a small irrigation supply company, and a Bush-Cheney fund-raiser.

But did she tell Emma to brush Spencer's few baby teeth? Did she remember to write down when she's bringing her son to the neighborhood moms-and-tots get-together? *We wish we could do this every week,* everyone agreed the last time all their schedules meshed—six months ago.

I've had so many clients in Janette's business, I've got a pretty good handle on what her days are like: She's up by five on a good day, searching her closets for the right weight suit and matching shoes she won't trip in, doing a few loads of laundry so Emma won't feel too put upon. She puts a few sticky notes for Emma near the phone: *Kiddie camp in Georgetown. Get us on the list! Hanna's birthday present. Any ideas? Go to Tree Top Toys.*

The crucial part of Janette's morning ritual is getting ready for the camera, no easy feat after Spencer has interrupted her beauty sleep several times and then David called in the middle of the night from Singapore. Since her male producers judge women far more harshly than they do members of their own sex, she's always under scrutiny.

Is her hair too long or too blond or too poufy this week? Is motherhood making her thirty-five years look more like fifty? Does she look ingénue enough to attract the younger-audience share, but "maturely intelligent" enough to keep the over-twenty crowd tuned in? If, for any reason, someone high up doesn't "like her look," she could be replaced in a heartbeat.

Yes, it's the twenty-first century. And, yes, female newscasters still compete in a perpetual Miss America contest. It doesn't matter how brilliant Janette Huntington is or how authoritatively she enlightens her viewers. It's *still* about how she looks for the stand-up.

Is Janette an "anchorette babe" in the making, or not?

Even Emma sounds flustered when I speak to her. Her employer flew in and out of the house three times this morning. When she was about to get into the car, she heard Spencer screaming. He spent the weekend with both his parents, so the Monday-morning transition to Emma wasn't as smooth as usual.

"They always do that at his age," Emma tells me. "I told Janette to just leave and we'd be fine, but she kept coming back into the house to try to calm him down, and it just made him angrier when she left again."

Then Janette's car was out of gas, so Emma helped her find David's car keys. (Good thing he wasn't driving it.)

When I catch Janette on the morning news, I can't believe how *collected* she seems after that kind of morning.

But that night she came home after ten, utterly despondent: Something happened in Afghanistan and they scrapped her healthcare story. She should have spent the day with Spencer, who has a really bad cold.

I can imagine Janette's thoughts: *Work's not going well—and I'm a lousy mother, too.*

Meanwhile, it's no secret that David, who used to love his work, is starting to fray. Things were supposed to smooth out once he made partner, but the honor just means bigger headaches. He's always jet-lagged and disoriented, and he knows he used to be a nicer guy. He can't remember what kind of flowers his wife likes (anemones or white roses?) or where they keep Spencer's extra diapers. He falls asleep at dinner. Calls from other time zones wake him and his wife and child at all hours. It used to be exciting to work in Bangkok, Tokyo, and South Africa, but he'd rather get to know his son and catch a movie with Janette.

Breaking news on the weather front: Hurricane Jane, David's mother, is coming to town. Batten down the hatches. Even Emma is starting to worry. That's what Janette and David were arguing about last night. "It won't be as bad as the last time," he says. Janette knows better. "I'll make it up to you," he promises.

16.

HOUSES OF CARDS

I T'S GREAT WHEN Grandma comes to town—especially if she's *your* mother. According to some of my clients, however, your mother-in-law can be another story. My friend Joanne gets along fabulously with her totally fun, great-with-the-children mother-in-law, and I'm sure you adore your husband's mother as well. But according to the most recent White House Nanny poll, many other women don't share your luck.

These Washington mothers are coping with demanding careers; their husbands' and children's equally time-crunched, complicated lives; the house, car, taxes, vacation, and—what really sends families over the edge—the dreaded third-grade science project.

Then in the middle of all this, your husband's mom decides to set you straight when she notices that your five-year-old needs a haircut: "Well, I suppose we did things *differently,*" she says with a forced chuckle, hardly disguising what she really means: *You're doing a lousy job with my grandchildren.*

One client's mother-in-law, a navy wife, raised four shipshape children by running their lives as efficiently as a military campaign. Every time the Commander was transferred to another base, she found, furnished, and organized another house in another state.

Did I mention that this grandmother didn't work outside *any* of those homes? Her daughter-in-law's a charming, highly respected public official. Her husband and three terrific children adore her, but Grandmother doesn't feel the same way. The spices aren't alphabetized, the sheets aren't ironed, and the playroom looks as if the children have been playing in it. Grandma's houses always passed the white-glove test.

Her son's wife is a slacker.

"I just cleaned your filthy, dirty refrigerator," Mrs. Second-in-Command announced during her last visit. "Which neither you *nor* your nanny has found time to do."

Adding injury to insult, this same grandmother invited her son, his children, and the *nanny* to join her for a week at Disney World. She didn't invite the children's mother. "Don't take it personally," her husband told her. "My mother thinks you want a little break from the children."

In February? When the rest of her family's swimming?

The majority of my clients live far away from what was once home, and their parents only streak into town as often as comets. The helpful grandparents throw themselves into cooking, cleaning, and fixing, and into playing with and reading to the children. Other kinds of grandparental visits are less memorable.

David, Janette, and Emma are bracing themselves; Hurricane Jane blows in on a Thursday. Even Spencer knows something serious is about to happen. The last time David's mother visited was right after their first nanny announced she was pregnant. Jane has never stopped reminding everyone that she always *knew* Donna wasn't going to work out.

No domestic diva, Janette will never live up to Jane's expectations. She hasn't organized her photo albums, and Spencer's toys are all over the place. But now that she has Emma, she's determined to pass muster. Emma had the dishwasher fixed and the cars detailed; she straightened out the linen closet and bought Jane's favorite imported oatmeal—and her prunes.

David just got back from a week in Asia. As soon as he unpacks, he has to go back to Dulles to meet his mother's flight. *Why does she always arrive at rush hour?* "Go to Dean and DeLuca," Janette tells Emma. "I don't care what it costs—thank God for their helpful prepared-food manager—tell everyone I'll get home in time for dessert."

Emma irons a tablecloth and sets the table. She serves pecan-crusted pork tenderloin, risotto cakes, and sugar snap peas; she made the salad dressing from scratch. "I guess cooking is a lost art in this house," Jane sighs. No fooling her; she's known for her discerning palate.

Janette rushes through the door just in time to hear Grandma ask Spencer, "Is Mommy working late again, Darling?"

When Emma sits down to eat with the family, Jane is shocked. *Her* help ate in a different room, from separate dishes. Janette and David consider their nanny a virtual member of the family, but she's just "the help" to Jane.

This hits a nerve in everyone.

You don't use cloth diapers? Is he warm enough in that thin sweater? You let him crawl around on the floor near the dog's bowl? Isn't he on a schedule? Our visiting dignitary is a master of the rhetorical question. Nothing Janette *or* Emma does is right: *David was toilet-trained at Spencer's age, and his articulation was much clearer. All my children went to sleep as soon as they were put down.*

As if Emma isn't busy enough making and serving Grandma breakfast and lunch—besides all her regular duties, Jane likes to be driven around. "Emma dear, if it isn't too much trouble, can we go to Saks Fifth Avenue?"

Shades of *Driving Miss Daisy.*

"No problem," Emma says, cheerily. She'll get through this.

Jane's happy to be with Spencer, but when it comes to the menial work, she lets Emma do it all while she basks in the glow. Grandma pushes the stroller for a few minutes in Montrose Park, and she reads stories to Spencer just long enough for photo ops. Emma washes spaghetti off the child, the walls, and the floors while Jane says how cute he looks. "Emma, have you seen my camera?" Translation: *Load it with film and take my picture with Spaghetti Boy. Quick.*

Many of my clients from very far away work for global organizations like the World Bank and the IMF. When their parents come, from China or India or Japan, they stay for weeks and sometimes months. These foreign grandparents, who aren't used to American child-rearing practices, often suffer the same culture shock our international nannies do. *The children don't respect their elders. The children are spoiled. The children have no manners.*

Those same remarks can be applied to their daughters-in-law as well, even though they try to do the right thing. "I was up in the middle of the night making *pooris* for my in-laws," an Indian FDA biostatistician complains. "They expect my nanny to wait on them, and they complain that I work too much instead of taking care of their son and grandchildren. I spend Saturdays taking them to Target, Costco, and Best Buy. All they like about this country is the shopping."

A highly competent nanny called me recently threatening to quit her job unless Grandma went back to Athens. "She thinks she's my supervisor! She was supposed to stay a few weeks, and now she's moving in for good! My boss can't wait to get out the door in the morning, but I'm stuck with her all day long."

Grandparents often have a lot of say about how their grandchildren are raised. When a Chinese-American couple requested a Mandarin-speaking nanny, I didn't think we had a prayer. Even though I've had occasional requests for one, I'd never placed a nanny who was fluent in Mandarin before.

We got lucky when Rose Hsu's application arrived just in time. She was highly educated and had been an engineer in China. Her husband was in D.C. to work for the National Institutes of Health, and her daughter went to the Wharton School of Finance.

The couple were thrilled with Rose's impressive credentials. But there was one more hurdle to this placement: Po Po (honorable Grandmother) was coming to town to make sure the prospective nanny's Mandarin was up to her standard.

What would we have done if Rose had flunked her Mandarin exam?

One of my best friends had her first child prematurely, and she held her baby like a fragile object. "Babies don't break," the Italian grandmother insisted. She pulled the baby's feet up to her ears when she was a week old, first one leg and then the other, saying, "We need to stretch her muscles." My friend's heart was in her throat.

Grandma had raised five children in this rough-and-tumble

manner, and her son and daughter-in-law were supposed to do the same. "She saw me straining some applesauce and laughed. She'd have given Gina lasagna when she was four months old. I told my nanny not to let the baby out of her *sight* when my mother-in-law's around."

There are many schools of child-rearing, but your in-laws probably went to a different one than you did: *Don't put the baby on her stomach. Heat up the formula. Get him on a rigid schedule. Why do the children need to take so many lessons?*

And your mother-in-law must know what she's talking about, because she raised the perfect son—the one you married.

Those District couples whose parents ease their parental burdens instead of making them worse have hit the jackpot. Especially if the grandparents live nearby and help out on a regular basis. When parents can't be their children's primary caregivers, grandparents are certainly better than outsourcing the entire job.

Many a nanny is able to work because *her* mother, who moved here from El Salvador or Bolivia or Brazil, watches the nanny's own children. When Bintu from Gambia came to me looking for a job, she had a seventeen-year-old, a fifteen-year-old, seven-year-old twins, and a two-year-old. Her references said she'd never missed a day of work, thanks to her mother. In fact, her client's children loved to go home with Bintu and spend time with her family. No matter how overwhelmed I expected her to be, the always-smiling Bintu gave new meaning to the concept of multitasking.

Nannies treat our clients' children like their own, so it pains me to hear what some of them tell me: "She never asked about *my* children once in four years."

I always say working women have to help one another, but most of my clients don't want to hear it. "I'd prefer someone who doesn't have her own children," they tell me. They need guaranteed total coverage. What if the nanny has a childcare emergency? "My life is complicated enough. I don't want *her* life to be complicated, too." I hear this all the time.

"I need someone from seven-thirty to six," a mother tells me.

"Most live-out nannies have children of their own," I explain. "Could you have someone live in?"

"We do have the space, but we really like our privacy."

They don't want someone living in, but they also don't want someone who commutes too far and has to deal with traffic. Their nanny has to be a certain age, have no children, and speak flawless English. "I want someone with a great personality and a really good head on her shoulders who'll be fun for the children."

I just don't want her to have a life outside our home. We laugh. These clients want the no-life nanny. *What if your boss decided not to hire you for the same reason?* I want to ask.

"I'd feel really bad having someone leave their child to take care of mine," I'm told. But the excellent nanny needs the job to sustain herself and her family—just like they do.

Nannies balance their houses of cards as carefully as their employers do. One of my favorite nannies had the perfect job in Silver Spring, five minutes from her home in Aspen Hill. As soon as she could afford to buy her own home, she moved her family to Frederick, an hour away, where the housing was more affordable. Meanwhile, her employers decided they could afford to live in the city, closer to their jobs.

Now the nanny was commuting an hour and fifteen minutes to work—on a good day. Her employers still insisted she get to work by eight to take the children to school. That meant she had to leave for her job too early to put her own daughter on the school bus. If the nanny's mother hadn't come to the rescue, this match would have been history.

In the middle of troubleshooting that predicament, I get a call from a grandmother who's trying to help her daughter-in-law—a woman I know only too well. Suzanne Taylor is the overprotective, paranoid attorney I mistook, several nannies ago, as a dream client. The last nanny I sent her didn't pass the tryout, but she finally hired someone I pray can handle such a neurotic mother.

"Please make this work," the elder Mrs. Taylor implores me. "My son is a wonderful, brilliant man." (Aren't they all?) "Suzanne's an authority on intellectual property. She went to Princeton and Yale. But she's a little high-strung, and frankly, Barbara, I'm worried about Alexander. His mother took him to the psychiatrist! Do you think that's normal? He's only four months old!"

We know who needed that appointment.

But grandmothers can be persuasive, so I called the Taylors' new nanny to give her a little pep talk and reassure her that Suzanne would calm down eventually. I hope I'm right.

Back on Wilton Road, the bad-weather weekend is taking its toll on everyone—especially Emma. "Everything goes so smoothly when *Janette's* parents visit," she tells me. "I've never met anyone quite like Mrs. Wilder."

"Do you think they really need this dog?" Jane keeps asking the nanny.

"I'm off to take Spencer to Messy Play," she says, glad to escape. When Jane finds out her son and his wife send their child to another organized activity, she has a field day.

"When my children were that age, I gave them a stick and a pail and let them dig worms in the backyard. Now you have to pay so your children can get dirty?" The nanny and Spencer are almost out the door, but now Jane thinks Spencer should finally wear that outfit she sent him. She's noticed the tag is still on it.

Emma changed him into his play clothes as soon as they were out of view, then changed him back again before they got home. Grandma never found out, but she did notice Emma eating a roast-beef sandwich from Sutton Gourmet after she stopped there to get Spencer a cookie. Had she charged that sandwich to Grandma's son?

If Jane knew how much Emma earns, she'd have cardiac arrest.

But Emma muddles through, thanks to her stiff-upper-lip endurance. She'll be out of here by Friday night. The weekend never looked so good to her.

Saturday is family day—after David watches Spencer for a few hours in the morning so Janette can finish some work. "I thought your wife was taking time off to be with us," Jane mutters. David has mastered the art of handling his mother, so she doesn't get to him. He simply agrees with her, no matter what she says, which drives Janette wild.

"Just ignore her," he repeats his mantra, driving his wife even wilder.

Janette spends her time at home in the den, out of the line of fire, with the latest White House document dump as her excuse to be alone. She finally, reluctantly closes her laptop to join her family for the big excursion to Discovery Creek, where Spencer learns to tunnel like an earthworm in the Children's Garden.

When it starts to drizzle, Jane sees no point in staying, even though everyone else is having a great time. Janette swears under her breath and David sympathizes. Spencer howls, but Grandma wins.

"He's getting tired anyway."

In another attempt to make Jane happy, a weekend sitter has been booked for Saturday night so the adults can go out. ("Emma lives here. What do you mean she doesn't work on weekends?" Jane wants to know.) Still trying to please an Unpleasable, David and Janette take Jane to dinner at Oceanaire because she likes seafood.

"Lovely meal. Awfully expensive," Jane laments. She also complains about the noise.

If Emma and Janette weren't truly bonded before Jane Wilder's visit, they certainly are by now.

17.

CAN I CHARGE
FOR THIS?

Yes, I spend a lot of time listening to clients' very specific requests for customized childcare, and just as much time interviewing and evaluating nannies.

But what I *really* do all day long and even some nights is run the White House Nannies Counseling Service. Feel free to listen in:

"*Of course* you should be able to take your bra off when you get home," I assure a client who simply wants to be comfortable at the end of her twelve-hour work day.

"I put on my sweats to watch *Access Hollywood,*" she says, coming to a slow boil. "Then our nanny and her boyfriend marched into the den and switched the channel to the Orioles! We said we want her to feel welcome here, but—"

"You didn't mean quite *that* welcome," I commiserate.

A lot of these therapeutic calls have to do with blurred employer-employee boundaries. "Our nanny likes to join us on

Sunday morning in her baby-doll pajamas. Yesterday she suggested we all play Monopoly. Then she took our *TV Guide* and circled all the programs she wants us to watch together."

Counseling can mean just listening, and that's what I did.

"I don't know how to tell you this." I hear that line a lot, but this time a nanny doesn't know what to do about a boss who steps over the line. It seems that the blue-suited, buttoned-down mom is going through a nasty divorce. She held herself together all day at the FCC but fell completely apart when she got home. She was so despondent about her husband's affair, she crawled into her nanny's bed for some sisterly consolation.

I can usually think of something to say, but this call stops me in my tracks. I know—what about a lock on the nanny's door?

When there are misunderstandings, I advise everyone to find time to sit and talk things out. Living with strangers can be tricky, and clear, honest communication is essential. But easier said than done. A nanny's afraid to ask her employers not to shout on Sunday mornings—her only morning to sleep in. A father can't understand why the nanny never puts gas in the car, and a mother isn't crazy about the dirty dishes in the nanny's room.

Occasionally all systems break down and nannies and families have to part company. When I hear those stories, I'm often tempted to ask the nanny or the family or both: *What were you waiting for?*

"I might have to hire a different nanny," a client says. Her children think they're being poisoned by the apparently mean-spirited woman who's run the family's lives for *twelve years.* After they named their children and chose their private schools, the nanny picked up where they left off. They were much too dependent on her to fire her, even though the children were complaining. When the nanny came to pick the kids up at school, they didn't want to get into the car. The situation got so bad that the school psychologist called the parents and suggested they make a personnel change.

True story.

Another client confessed she was having nightmares about being *murdered* by her nanny. The woman was educated and opinionated—okay, a bit controlling—and their close relationship turned into a clash between the two strong-willed women. But murder? Another case of Time to Move On.

"Tell me I'm not crazy, but we've had to let her go," another client reports.

I'm thinking *Halleluiah! They've seen the light,* but I don't say it. That relationship was always volatile. When the family got a new car, the live-out nanny was livid that they traded in their old car instead of giving it to her. She'd shout at her employers for any reason. And she had the nerve to inform them they weren't taking proper care of their children's teeth.

The dad in that family was a dentist.

The same nanny also took the liberty of donating a high chair and other furniture to the next-door neighbors because she thought they needed it more. The final straw was when she rescued some very old restaurant leftovers from the trash and served it to the children for dinner.

I guess it was easier than cooking them a brand-new meal.

This nanny worked in a prime nanny-poaching section of Arlington, where there are so many nannies that mothers, desperate for childcare, cruise the parks and playgrounds for unhappy ones to entice. Anyone who spotted that nanny taking food from the garbage can would have thought she was so mistreated they'd be able to hire her away in a minute. They would have been sorry if they had.

Still, the employers gave that nanny a raise, and even took her with them on vacation. "She's so good with our children," the mother told me. I guess it didn't matter how the nanny treated her and her husband. But eventually, I'm glad to say, they called to ask me for another nanny.

Maybe I should run a support group for clients—or nannies— who love too much.

I even make counseling house calls. A client in Maryland needed help as soon as possible. "I don't trust my judgment," she kept repeating. The elegant, ultracompetent wife of a prominent Bush One Republican managed her home and four children beautifully.

For some reason, the last nanny who worked in that stately Chevy Chase Village home—certainly not one of our placements—had eroded this client's self-confidence. I soon understood why. When it was time to get rid of the Christmas tree, Vera the nanny insisted on dragging it out to the curb, even though her employer said it was too heavy for her. Suddenly the nanny was gasping for air and clutching her chest.

"I thought she was having a heart attack," the client told me. "I called the Rescue Squad, but Vera got hysterical and begged me not to let them come. Of course I had no choice. The paramedics had to restrain her, and when they got down to the business of examining her, she started to scream."

She was a he.

This client is nothing if not smart. "Our nanny's been with us for over a year," she groaned. "How could I not have known?"

Was this an early version of *Mrs. Doubtfire*?

During the Clinton Administration, a writer dad who worked at home was in the middle of an ongoing battle between two high-maintenance women. His wife was a condescending White

House employee. Their nanny, a chic Spanish woman with lots of presence, was sensitive to any kind of criticism and a bit hard to direct.

"My wife's a micromanager," the father admitted. "Sure the nanny's a bit difficult, but I'm here every day and I know she's doing a terrific job with Jonathan. She'd throw herself in front of a bus for him. What am I supposed to do?"

I let him talk for a while until he felt better. His peacemaking skills had worked so far, but his wife was about to stay home on maternity leave with their second child. "You're right," I said, "those two women can't be under the same roof."

It's hard to choose which of my patients—I mean clients—to add to this collection. One couple was definitely in the almost-crazy category, and maybe not "almost" after their just-as-crazy nanny pushed them over the edge. She defied the parents at every opportunity. If they told her "No McDonald's for the children," it was Happy Meals for everyone. The nanny had been told not to take the children to the zoo, but she took them anyway. The parents tried to reach her seventeen times, but she'd "forgotten" to turn her cell phone on.

Okay, so this nanny was textbook passive-aggressive. The mother's reaction, however, takes the cake. When the nanny got home from the zoo, the mother was holding up a sign that said DO NOT TALK. DO NOT SAY ANYTHING. Nanny was allowed to stay, but only with the understanding that, as soon as the mother came in the door, she wasn't allowed to talk to the children. She was on mute. We have pages of notes about this placement. Whenever the nanny got into trouble, she called me to recount her latest infraction. "You know better. Why do you keep doing that stuff?" I'd ask.

"IknowIknowIknowIknowIknow . . ." she'd say.

"So if you know, then cut it out," I replied.

Can I call this psychotherapy? Can I bill as if it is?

All these emotional emergencies fall into basic categories. First, there are the anxiety-driven premature calls from women pregnant with their first child. "Sure, send in the application," I tell them. "But until you actually have that baby, you may not know what kind of help you really need."

The next stage of advice-giving is helping new parents figure out that perhaps they don't need a nanny with perfect language skills or an advanced degree in child psychology to take wonderful care of their newborn. I listen to them theorize about what kind of person they want. After they interview a few nannies, they'll realize they really want someone who knows innately how to comfort and care lovingly for their infant, even if she lacks academic credentials.

There are two schools of nannies, I always explain. Some are formally educated, and some just have years of experience. There are great caregivers in both categories.

A lot of highly accomplished women feel totally overwhelmed by their brand-new seven-pound dictators and clueless about taking care of them. I assure each one that no new mom was more ignorant than I was, so I understand their feelings of helplessness.

Once a nanny's finally hired, my next job is to help employers and employees get through the sometimes-difficult adjustment period. Parents ask a zillion questions: What can and can't they ask the nanny to do? Should they let the nanny bring her child to work? Occasionally a mother calls on Day Three to say, "We made a mistake."

"You loved her," I remind the panicky client. "She has great references. Talk to her. And let's give it a little more time and see how it goes." Two weeks later, all is well.

A nanny might call me when she's homesick, or to complain that she feels taken for granted because the parents forgot it was her birthday or don't want to pay her when they decide to take a vacation.

I am the voice of reason.

But sometimes, even I'm stumped.

A venture capitalist and his attorney wife implicitly trusted the married, live-out nanny they'd had for six years. Small bills seemed to be disappearing from the mother's wallet, but it must have been her imagination as it couldn't have been the nanny. But after she planted a $20 bill next to her purse, it was gone the next morning. Her nanny was the only possible culprit.

The client was beside herself. She and her husband had already accepted the nanny's gracious invitation for dinner at her home, so they went. The nanny's husband opened the door, wearing a polo shirt which was obviously *not* his; the employer's privately held company logo was embroidered on the pocket. My clients were so speechless they could barely get through the hors d'oeuvres. "And then, when we sat down, I realized *my* Irish linen tablecloth was on *her* table!"

That nanny had always gotten rave reviews and was considered magic with young children. Who knew she had other tricks up her sleeve, like making things disappear? I almost laughed, the story was so preposterous; but the professional in me wanted to come up with an explanation.

"Clearly she wants to be caught," was my amateur attempt at Freudian analysis. Why else would you dress your husband and your table in stolen goods? When I asked how my client wanted to deal with the situation, she still didn't know.

I didn't know, either. Just like a flummoxed therapist, I called my friend Martha, the psychiatric social worker, for help. "Don't judge them for their blind dependency," Martha said. "But help them cut the cord."

P.S. The nanny stayed.

And finally, I promise, I have to include the client who was mortified when her new nanny insisted there were bugs in her bedroom. The embarrassed parents had just moved into an older home in Baltimore and, even though they didn't see any insects, they called the exterminators immediately. The nanny took all her clothes to the dry cleaner's and her employers had all the carpets steam-cleaned. Two weeks later the nanny was still waking the pregnant mother in the middle of the night, swatting, slamming, and stomping the insects in her attic room. She barely had energy to care for the child during the day.

This was a client I adored and wanted to help. I'd handselected this nanny because I was sure she'd be great. She'd worked for three physician couples in a row, and she had beautiful references. Even my client's hard-charging mother had approved this choice.

The house was sprayed so many times that the mother was terrified they'd all get sick from the toxins. But it turned out that the only bugs in that house were the ones in the nanny's head. Yikes.

No charge for all my hours of social work putting that client back together.

David and Janette are finally back together, as well. Now that his mother has gone and left destruction in her wake, David's thanking his wife with a real splurge: dinner and an overnight at the Inn at Little Washington. It's a world-class destination an hour and a half away in the foothills of the Blue Ridge Mountains. Where no cell-phone service roams.

It's the first time Emma will be on overnight duty alone.

Some parents leave their nannies home to mind the children for days and nights on end, but Janette and David have decided never to be away at the same time. This occasion calls for an exception to the rule; Spencer's almost two, and they'll only be gone one night. Emma insists it's a great idea for them to go. Finally, that romantic tryst they didn't get to have in Virgin Gorda. No Spencer this time. No sunburned nanny. No Grandma.

Janette has been superproductive lately, and the producers in New York are pleased with her audience share, so she's earned a little getaway. David always has to be reachable no matter where he is, but he assures her that all his cases are in great shape and that no one will try.

They barely get through the first few courses of their late dinner. Port-braised veal sweetbreads for David and quartered suckling Pyrénées lamb with new carrots and cress meunière for Janette. While they're waiting for dessert, the waiter brings David a message, which cannot be good news. He excuses himself to find a land line, and when he comes back he can't look his wife in the eye.

He has to get to a meeting tomorrow—in Hawaii.

"Here's the good news. We still get to spend the night together. Here's the other news: I have to be at Dulles by seven."

"That's just *great*," Janette says through gritted teeth.

Can David expense this almost-ruined thousand-dollar fiasco to his client?

18.

CAR TALK

OUR NATION'S CAPITAL is magnificent. Navy architect and engineer Pierre-Charles L'Enfant laid out the city of Washington with grand avenues radiating from Parisian-like traffic circles. Just don't try to drive in it. I've been living here my entire adult life, and I still approach Chevy Chase Circle with terror in my heart.

How many times have I heard the story about the nanny who drove around and around Dupont Circle? Just like the dad in *European Vacation,* she couldn't figure out how to get off and never returned. The reason for all the confusion is obvious. L'Enfant designed D.C. a hundred years before there were automobiles— or nannies driving them.

Maybe you've seen their license plates: 4RNANNY, NANCAR, DCNANNY. Don't forget: After you've bought the top-of-the-line carriage, stroller, jogging stroller, and car seat for your child, there's one more baby-transportation expense: the nanny car. How will your child get from one place to another? *What car will the nanny drive?*

We make sure our caregivers have excellent driving records, but even so, some of my clients go into shock when they realize they'll have to let the nanny drive their vehicle.

I don't know what to do, I hear all the time. "Sometimes I drive the Lexus to work and my husband always takes the Explorer. Then there's the Alfa, but that's hardly a *nanny* car . . ."

Let me get this straight: They leave their children in her care, and they're worried about the *car*—which they can replace?

Some nannies do have their own cars, but it's not always a vehicle you'd want to put your child in. Happy are the clients whose nanny drives up in a brand-new minivan. They don't have to buy her a car? She gets the job. I was thrilled when one of my own nannies arrived in a mint-condition Mercedes. But she was afraid my children would get her car dirty, so she wouldn't let them in it.

Some of my clients hand over their car keys quite easily. One mother even trusted her young Scottish nanny with a Seven Series BMW (minimum price tag, fifty grand). Then she answered her doorbell one night and saw a policeman holding an object that was hard to recognize out of context. I mean, out of the car.

"We thought you might want this back," the officer said. When he explained that it was her *glove compartment,* she was still in denial until her registration, her child's binky, and some of her husband's golf tees fell out of it.

It was lucky that the nanny was fine, because the rest of that lovely BMW was wrapped around a tree. Did they fire the lass? Well, she was *so* wonderful with their children, and her accent was so charming that those employers decided to relieve her of the driving duties and keep her on.

Another client was a lot less understanding about an accident that wasn't even her nanny's fault. She'd been happy with the nanny for a long time, so when she gave her a lukewarm reference, I called to find out why. "Cynthia was wonderful," I was told. "But right before she left, she damaged our Audi. She said she was sorry, but frankly, Barbara, she just didn't seem sorry *enough*."

I wanted to know about Cynthia's childcare performance so I could help her get another position, but all I heard about was that Audi. Cynthia had never had an accident before, and she'd been driving in the rain on Georgetown Pike, a windy, treacherous road even on a sunny day. No one was hurt, and in fact the police commended the nanny for avoiding a much worse accident.

"Did my boss tell you she wanted me to lie to the insurance company about who was driving?" Cynthia asked me. "Did she tell you the tires were completely bald?"

So after their nanny had given those employers two years of great service, they were too upset about their thousand-dollar deductible to give her the good reference she deserved.

Richard and I spotted my best friend's English nanny's Oldsmobile coming straight at us on the wrong side of Bradley Boulevard. Did Claire forget she wasn't driving around Liverpool? I don't believe in minding my friends' nanny business, especially since I hadn't placed Claire in the first place. But safety first, so this time I reported the incident.

Parents experience traffic traumas, too. Sometimes they cause them. Back to Suzanne Taylor, who wanted her nanny to come with her while she drove around Bethesda, the only way she can put her child to sleep. According to the alarmed nanny, every time Alexander whimpered, Suzanne turned around to comfort the child. "Then she came to a dead stop in the middle of River

Road," the nanny continues the saga. The baby had dropped his binky, and Mommy insisted on finding it. "I kept saying, 'Let me do that,' but she insisted on finding the pacifier herself!"

I can picture this all too well: Suzanne stopped dead in the middle of the six-lane road, surrounded by honking, justifiably road-enraged drivers. Because Alexander needed his binky.

Priorities.

Our nannies get lost in D.C. far more often than they get into fender-benders. We're always sympathetic. My husband, who moved here when he was two (not quite a native), knows every shortcut and alternative route from anywhere to anywhere else in metropolitan Washington, so all logistical questions go to him. When a nanny's stuck in a Beltway backup on her way to work, Richard takes the frantic call.

I can always tell when he's talking to a lost nanny: "See the church on the right? You don't see it? Keep going. Okay. Now make a left at the Exxon station. Keep going. No, not the Mobil, the Exxon . . ."

Meanwhile, I've talked to three clients, but Richard's still making sure that same nanny gets off at the right exit and can find her employer's house. He's especially good at calming down caregivers from tropical places like Fiji and the Seychelles who aren't used to driving on snowy roads. "Just relax, Farnita. You can do this. I know you can."

Excellent advice to all new nannies: Do a practice drive before you need to go anywhere—not that this always does the trick. The day before my nanny Pam started working for me, I took her on a dry run to my daughter's preschool. The distance from our house to Abingdon Montessori School is 2.5 miles, with two traffic circles to be navigated. Her estimated travel time was eight minutes; ten, tops.

Pam should have been back home with Gillian by noon. But when I called to hear about my daughter's first day of school, there was no answer. The teacher said Pam had picked Gillian up on time, so I called home every five minutes for the next forty, then called the neighborhood police. Then I got in my car to hunt them down. Fortunately, I had a car phone in 1990, so Richard called as soon as he heard from Pam. She and Gillian were fine. They were in a run-down industrial section near the Baltimore Inner Harbor, an hour away.

Blame it on L'Enfant. Pam had taken the wrong spur off Westmoreland Circle onto Massachusetts Avenue. Within a few miles she was on Embassy Row: Great Britain on her right, Finland on her left, etc. When nothing looked familiar, she stopped and asked a man coming out of the Peruvian embassy. Maybe he was thinking about the streets of Lima, because he sent Pam to Chevy Chase by way of Baltimore.

I've mentioned my nanny Kayla, who burned out our vintage Mercedes engine, and Pam, who was lost more often than she was found. But as soon as my children grew up and got their own licenses, I was sorry I couldn't hire a nanny to drive them around anymore. Matt racked up a half-dozen moving violations, the last one on the day he left for college. Just to ensure that our separation wouldn't be quite so painful. Entrapments, speed traps, he didn't hit that car, he only gave it a love tap. Was it *his* fault he ran out of quarters and missed the meter maid by five lousy minutes?

Matt got tickets in the District, Maryland, and Virginia, winning the traffic trifecta! We had to hire lawyers in all three jurisdictions. University of Michigan, here he comes—where the only wheels he'll have are the two on his bicycle.

It used to be adorable when Gillian tried to copy her big brother. Then she was voted Most Likely to Have an Accident by her senior class. Gillian thought this was "hilarious," and maybe it would have been—if she hadn't run into someone, who then ran into a school bus, the very next day.

The only good thing about racing from the Inn at Little Washington to Dulles Airport on Interstate 66 for David's early flight is the lack of traffic at six A.M. No lack of tension in the car, however.

"So much for that lobster omelet you promised me. Weren't you going to have the scrambled eggs with house-cured salmon, David? Or was it the brioche French toast with homemade blackberry sauce?"

Considering what had just happened to them, I can't imagine ordering anything with blackberries in it.

Janette can't resist a bit more ranting. She still has time to make their last hour together even more cathartic. "I have to admit you certainly fooled me when you picked a place with no cell-phone service, David. And by the way, you still owe me big-time for your mother."

There's silence in the car until David finally says what's on his mind.

"*How do you think I feel?* I have to get on another F-ing plane. The client just decided to pursue a merger, and I'm the only one in the firm who can sit with the managers and the bankers and formulate a strategy." Janette can't even look at him when he turns to her and asks, "Do you think this is easy for me?"

This never occurred to her. David's not the type to unload his emotional baggage, and it brings Janette up short. She can hardly read the signs to the airport through the tears filling her eyes.

"I know it's not your fault," she says before they kiss good-bye. "I'm just so disappointed."

When she finally gets home, Janette faces an unusual prospect: an entire, unplanned, free day. Even though she's a solo parent, once Emma leaves it'll be fun to spend some okay-it's-a-cliché quality time with her child.

"You're back already?" says Emma, who knows enough to be sympathetic.

"Don't ask. David's on his way to Hawaii."

The nanny rolls her eyes in female commiseration. She's done the same with David after Janette changed her family plans at the last minute. "I'm going to run to Strosniders," Emma says, changing the subject. "That leaky bathroom faucet is driving me potty. I'll get a washer and fix it myself."

God bless Emma. Pouring fat-free milk into her Cheerios, Janette thinks wistfully again about her quickly evaporated get-away. Did she dream she and David drank that Château Margaux '82, worth (almost) every penny? Did she even taste the chocolate-pistachio soufflé and the Seven Deadly Sins assortment?

Before Janette's finished feeding Spencer his Cheerios, Emma's back already. Someone broadsided her in Bradley Shopping Center. The pale and trembling nanny points to a bashed-up Volvo in the driveway; it's not totaled, but it does need major work.

"Emma, don't worry. You're fine, right? It's just a car, and we have insurance."

"The wanker was running his mouth on the mobile and smashed straight into me." This is the first time Janette has ever seen her nanny more stressed out than she is. "I should have seen that bloody twit coming," Emma fumes.

Janette makes Emma some tea and tells her to ask Charles to

pick her up. She makes a mental note to give Emma a gift certificate for a massage at Andre Chreky. She ought to get herself one there, too. Wasn't that on her To Do list? But Emma comes first. As my savviest clients know, *protect your nanny with your life.*

One family treated their nanny to a week in Paris at their *fantastique* apartment near the Eiffel Tower. A massage is great, but I'd take a week on the Left Bank.

More thoughts buzzed through our White House correspondent's overcharged brain: *Emma hasn't had a vacation. Did that have anything to do with this? Was the accident my fault? Where's David when I need him to deal? I don't even know which insurance company to call to report this. I'm glad David's gone because we need his car. Thank God Emma wasn't hurt, or Spencer, or anyone else . . .*

When Janette returns to the here and now, she realizes three things: First, her nanny's running out the door with her weekend bag packed. Second, her almost-two-year-old is pulling on her skirt, screaming, and his nose is running. "Where Emma? EMM-MMAAA!" And third, Ginger the still-not-housebroken puppy has peed on the floor again, and the puddle is spreading perilously close to Janette's Longchamp handbag where her cell phone and BlackBerry reside.

Couldn't Emma have walked Ginger before she left? Did she get Spencer new shoes? Where are they?

She can't reach David until he lands in Honolulu eight hours from now. In fact, she may not even be able to reach him there, since he had no idea which hotel he'd stay in after the meeting. His office is closed. BlackBerrys don't always work that well on airplanes. All communications are down for who knows how long. Her husband will be technically on U.S. soil and still—unreachable. She's so unnerved that she's working herself into a lather. *What if I really need to get him? What if Emma had been in a serious accident? What if she and Spencer had been* hurt?

Janette's next assignment—after she rescues her purse, the dog, and the child, in that order—is to figure out how to get through the day. She's in a rare kind of shock: alone with her child for the next several totally unplanned *hours.* Few of my clients ever experience this much downtime with their children. They're used to the fast lane, to constantly calibrating their minutes and seconds no matter how crazy their schedules get.

What throws them into a complete panic is when their inner clock stops ticking.

When a client hired one of our temporary nannies to give her child dinner on a weeknight, it didn't seem out of the ordinary. Until she told us she'd be having dinner as well. "My husband's traveling again," she explained. "I just like the company." Isn't her thirteen-year-old daughter company enough?

That tends to happen around here. So you'll understand why I congratulated the parents who decided to both stay home with their newborn for a few weeks—without *any* help. "Maybe we should experience what it's like to be alone with the baby," the husband said. Even though they're nervous, a trial by fire gives new parents the confidence to know they can do it alone. No matter what snafus await them during the next several years, they'll know they can survive. Total dependency on others is never a good idea, no matter how wonderful your childcare package is.

Janette squelches the fleeting thought to call our temp service and decides to fly solo for the day. She calls a few of her friends with children, but no one's free to play at the last minute. No problem. She and Spencer will have a special mother-and-son day. *I can do this,* she tells herself. Just like the Little Engine That Could.

Now, *What Would Emma Do? She'd Metro down to the Smithsonian so Spencer can visit the dinosaurs.*

Smithsonian, here we come.

I think I'll drive.

19.

FREQUENT FLYERS,
WHINERS, AND
WORRIERS

I MEET SUCH an enormous, colorful cast of characters in my business, I can never keep up with them all. And I don't have to, because a lot of them keep up with me. So, just in case, I keep their childcare needs (and their other needs as well) uppermost in my mind at every moment.

Remember Mr. Are You Thinking About Me? He's in great company. Let's take Zoe Littlefield, who not only *has* a three-year-old but *is* one as well. Every conversation with her starts with the same whiny question: "Is anyone paying attention to *me*?"

"Well, *now* we are," Karen says when she's lucky enough to get Zoe call. But this self-centered mom has taught us a great therapeutic technique. If someone in the office is having a hard time, we just take center stage, stamp our feet, and bellow, "No one's paying attention to *me*," and we all feel better.

"You know what a wonderful employer I am and how well I treat my help," Zoe reminds me. She wants her next nanny to speak French so her children can keep up their fluency. "We lived abroad, you know." We certainly know. And sure, Zoe, no problem. But the only available French-speaking nanny is from the Belgian Congo, and I don't think she'd fit your profile.

The Littlefields live close to me in Bethesda, in a lovely but hardly grandiose neighborhood of standard center-hall Colonials. After I heard Zoe describe her home as "palatial" several times, I went on a little field trip one day to see her Taj Mahal, just to satisfy my curiosity.

Okay. The Littlefields did have the nicest house on the block, so that joke was on me. But despite their tempting nanny digs, no one wanted to work for this family. Was that because of Zoe's *noblesse oblige* attitude? Great house, but who wants to be there when the Queen is always in residence?

Bruce Madison's another frequent flyer. To refresh your memory, he's the divorced CEO with enough government contracts to keep his exes in the style they're accustomed to. Moira the part-time nanny takes care of Bruce's part-time daughters, and she says the job would be fine if it weren't for Dad's Prada-wearing, full-time girlfriend, Lisette.

"He just gave her a *huge* engagement ring," Moira reported when she dropped in at the office for another heart-to-heart talk. "I can't take it anymore. Now that the Manipulator's marriage campaign finally worked, she's really insufferable."

I listen sympathetically. Most nannies complain that they're not appreciated, but that's not Moira's problem. In fact, Bruce is so concerned about her that every time she even *thinks* about changing jobs, he catches her unspoken vibe and throws another

$10,000 a year in Moira's direction—for the twenty-hour-a-week, cushy job.

But this nanny's at the end of her rope anyway. "There aren't many part-time jobs in your price range," I remind this nanny. It's hard to leave a position when you're in "golden handcuffs," but Moira surprises me.

"The money isn't worth it," she insists. "The girls are in school most of the day, and I just don't feel useful enough. I want more of a sense of accomplishment from my job."

Moira takes temporary jobs in her spare time and has even worked for a major White House Insider. As Bruce Madison well knows, one of her other employers could snake his nanny away any day now.

A treasonous offense, of course. More about that later.

Let's just see what happens when Moira's offered half her salary for double the hours. Those handcuffs might seem pretty comfortable after all.

I like and respect the three hardworking Sri Lankan sisters I've placed with Washington families, but Malika, Nilanti, and Rampalee call a *lot*. As soon as I hear one of their unmistakable greetings: *"Babahrah?"* I brace myself for another shrill Sri Lankan download. (Who needs Caller ID?) The sisters don't get along with one another, so whoever calls always warns me not to tell the other two what she's calling about.

Not to worry, I can't remember which one is unhappy about which job, anyway! I listen yet again to twenty minutes of griping about the undisciplined children, unhousebroken pets, and spoiled parents one of the sisters has to put up with; then I repeat my classic, futile mantra: "Malika (or Nilanti or Rampalee)," I say, "Did you tell your boss what you're telling me?"

"Oh, *Bahbahrah*. I could *never* say this to her. Do you have another job for me?" Beg, beg. Plead, plead.

I know how difficult these women's situations are, and I'm certainly sympathetic, but no matter where they work, they'll need to speak up for themselves, so there's nothing I can do.

A policy analyst for the Brookings Institution also calls me regularly to complain because her nanny has changed the schedule again, or she wants another raise, three months after her last one. Now she wants to bring her child to work—on a day when her employers' children are in school.

"Do I have to pay my nanny to take care of her own child in *my* house? Sofie does a great job with the children, so I guess we'll help her out. But what do you think, Barbara?"

Whatever I say, I know she'll do whatever Sofie wants her to, so by now I've learned to just make this client feel all right about giving in. "Are your kids happy?"

"Yes."

"Is she doing a good job?"

"Yes."

"Do you really want to look for someone new?"

"No, not really. You're right. You're better than my therapist," she says, after we reach closure.

Now who can I complain to? And why isn't anyone paying attention to *me*?

Aside from all the complaint calls, real or imaginary, I hear frequently from nannies who are happy with their jobs and clients who are happy with their nannies. But, you know, the grass is always greener, so they're convinced they can still "do better."

Hi, Barbara. Yes, everything's wonderful. Chat, chat, chat. By the way, are there any new jobs/nannies I should know about?

"I'm just checking to see who's around," clients say. "You never know. What if our nanny moves to Alaska/goes back to school/gets married?"

"But none of those things has happened yet," I say. Parents who are satisfied with their childcare but call "just in case" should focus on more worrisome topics, such as global warming or the national debt. I often wonder how any work gets done in the town—besides my own, of course.

"You don't realize how lucky you are," I say. "You have one of the best nannies in Washington. *I could place her in a minute.*" As soon as I say those magic words, I can get back to the clients and nannies who really need my help.

T he Hampton Wick is on the line," Karen trills. That's Brit-speak for something that rhymes with "wick," I'm afraid. Jeffrey Darwin, aka Maserati Man, has yet another dilemma. His nanny says it's too hard for her to take his sons to school because she's busy with the baby.

"How can I possibly drive Ben and Eric to Landon?" Jeffrey asks me. "I'm running a ten-million-dollar company." He goes on and on for so long about how important his time is, I want to suggest that he simply hang up and drive his children to school. With his income, he could hire a second nanny, but I know better than to suggest it. Maserati Man already resents paying his one overworked nanny. By the time I'm through talking to Jeffrey, my jaw hurts from gritting my teeth.

. . .

Speaking of schools, two-year-old Spencer Huntington-Wilder will soon attend one of Washington's finest private preschools. After e-mailing all her peers, Janette applied to St. Margaret's, Chevy Chase Unitarian, and, her first choice, Capitol Child Academy. She and David spent way too much time slaving over the applications, which included a photograph of Spencer and an essay about him as well as a letter of recommendation from his music teacher.

Maybe Emma should write to the committee as well, assuring them that Spencer can listen to instructions, concentrate, finish tasks, and transition from one activity to the next. Janette and David provide information about their occupations and educations, as well as how long they've lived at their current address. These schools aren't exactly looking for economic diversity. Impressive parents, implicit donations.

One of my clients was told that the preschool admissions process could be *two years long* if her child didn't get in the first time around. When he was wait-listed for the second year in a row, she called to raise hell. The admissions officer was deeply apologetic. Of course her son was totally qualified, but the school had mistakenly put his application in the wrong folder with the first-year applicants. Even for preschools, it's vital to have a coded application in Washington, so as soon as that child had one, he or she was *in*.

Most White House Nannies work with children in this preschool demographic, so we're often intimately involved with the drama of it all. Even parents who are always on the lookout for a better nanny stop looking during interview season. Suddenly, all they are about is *stability*, so until that letter of acceptance arrives, nothing in their child's life can change.

"Please don't leave us now," parents implore their nannies. "We can't upset his emotional equilibrium during this crucial time. *We're applying to private school*."

It's white-knuckle time for Janette and David as well; they've got all the right stuff for CCA, and a neighbor of theirs is on the board and has volunteered to write a letter on Spencer's behalf— *de rigueur*. (Does she praise the child's fine motor skills? Does she mention that Spencer is kind to animals?)

When it comes to Admissions, it certainly helps to be "someone," but who isn't around here? Even after an exclusive incoming class has already been chosen, if you're a recently appointed official who's just moved to town, a slot often miraculously opens up.

If Spencer's anointed, his first step to the Ivy League will be well worth twelve thousand a year for five stimulating mornings a week from 8:45 to 11:50 (minus every vacation in the book). Don't forget the generous yearly contribution to the building fund.

But you just never know. David's Important Friend's child was perfectly scripted and performed beautifully in *her* play session, but she was *wait-listed*. This deeply dreaded news is often the kind way to reject a child so his or her parents can save face.

You may never know why your child wasn't among the chosen, but you can speculate. One clueless couple asked their *nanny* to take their son to an "observation session," which was, I suspect, an easy no for the admissions board. I don't envy these committees the task of choosing among children who are all from the right families.

My friend Joanne's son Zack didn't get into Beauvoir because he hid under a table and held on to his mother's leg during the entire hour interview. *Can your child take instruction? Can he separate? Is he socially ready to be part of a group?* I guess the answer in Zack's case was no.

When I first took Matt for his kindergarten interview at Maret School, I admit I was a little anxious. My three-year-old was a loose cannon. Could he last forty minutes without getting himself into trouble? In case you think it was my idea, they *tell* you to bribe your child so he'll perform his very best when he's being evaluated. (No, I don't know who "they" are.)

So if your child doesn't always behave like royalty, go ahead. When that fateful day arrives, promise him or her anything: a motorized Mercedes just like Daddy's or a spa day with Mommy.

The Maret School was such an appealing place, and the kindergarteners have their own charming house on the campus. Matt returned from his Observed Play Time smiling from ear to ear, totally satisfied with himself.

"Now I want my ice-cream cone," he said.

Yes, I promised him ice cream at ten-thirty in the morning. Let this be an inspiration to you when it comes to bribery: Be creative. So we stopped at Swenson's for two chocolate cones. As we were walking to the car, I asked Matt if he'd seen Mrs. Gold, the Lower School director of admissions. "Yeah, I saw her," he said, happily licking his cone. "Mrs. Gold told me not to do karate chops."

"She told you what, Matt?" I almost swerved into the cars parked along Connecticut Avenue.

"I did a karate chop on Jason. He was a jerk," my son informed me matter-of-factly. I guess he wanted to show his future classmates who was the alpha male. And he'd been smart enough not to breathe a word of this until after that forbidden morning ice cream was melting down his chin.

Shouldn't that astuteness have qualified him for any school?

P.S. Matt made the Maret waiting list and was happy ever after at the Potomac School. When his sister, Gillian, applied there four years later, they gave her cardboard shapes to fit together into triangles and circles to test her spatial relations. I flunked when I tried to put those shapes together, and so did she. No problem. Gillian was so verbal she'd shine in the next part of the interview.

"What's a castle?" she was asked. Gillian has always been a big talker, but suddenly my four-year-old was mute. Her interviewer called me into the room to see what was going on: For the first (and last) time in her life, my daughter had nothing to say.

But as soon as I got her out of there, Gillian told me all about castles: *That's where the princess lives. And the prince comes to visit her. Castles are high and pointy, and they have big flags and water all around them.* . . . Thank God for the sibling-gets-in policy, because she made it in the end.

When Emma returns from her weekend, the house looks like a bomb went off in it. Monday-morning messes are huge nanny complaints, and even mild-mannered Emma is fuming. Newspapers and dirty dishes are everywhere, Spencer has no clean clothes, the puppy needs to be walked immediately, and she knows she'll find puppy poo where it's not supposed to be. *If I'd left the house like this, I'd have been fired,* Emma thinks. *Talk about a double standard. You'd think Janette should get the Congressional Medal of Honor for taking care of her own child and puppy for a day and a half.*

She wanted to go to the park, but instead she has to clean the house. And there's no food in the house because Janette forgot to call Peapod, so Emma has to take Spencer with her to the super-market. While standing on a painfully slow line at the Westbard Giant, Emma's stuck behind a woman and her howling baby.

"I'm really sorry. She's so fussy this morning," says the obvi-ously new mom.

"Oh, let me see the baby," Emma says, distracting the infant, who immediately settles down and smiles at her. Emma has al-ways been magic with babies.

"How did you do that?" the mother asks her. "Is that your adorable little boy?"

"No, I'm his nanny. Spencer, say hello."

"Hi, Spencer. My name is Ellen Winter. What's your nan-ny's name?"

"*EMMA!*" Spencer shouts, as if introducing his nanny.

"Hi, Emma. Boy, do I need someone like you. Are any of your friends looking for a job?"

After the morning I just had, I *could be looking,* Emma thinks, sur-prising herself. *Maybe I just need a vacation.*

Standard operating procedure for procuring a nanny in the District of Columbia: Opportunity can strike anywhere, at any moment. You think you've sent your nanny to buy eggs and the next thing you know—she's *poached.*

"You're not by chance looking for a new job, are you, Emma?" The nanny smiles, but doesn't bite.

"I'll look for you at Turtle Park," Emma's new friend calls out as they part company. And then she does the working-woman thing (even on maternity leave) and hands Emma her card.

A nanny like Emma is approached often, sometimes even by her employers' friends. Losing a wonderful nanny can happen in-nocently enough. A nanny who's been a substitute teacher at your child's preschool may be offered a wonderful job there. Nannies often leave jobs to go back to school, or get married and have their own children. But, sad to report, the heinous crime of nanny-napping, the equivalent of high treason, seems to happen in this competitive town more frequently than anywhere else.

The most despicable form of this crime is the nanny theft that occurs too close to home: in your neighborhood or at your children's school. You never know who's stalking your nanny in the carpool line or at the community pool. When parents call to report this theft, they feel utterly betrayed. Think of your husband leaving you for your best friend. The children feel betrayed, too: *Why is my nanny taking care of someone else?*

Nasty business.

When nannies leave to take a different job, and distraught parents ask, "What can I tell my child?" I suggest an innocent white lie: *Silvia had to go back to Chile to be with her own children.* But when a four-year-old sees her former nanny caring for another child on a daily basis, that lie doesn't work. How could anyone be so oblivious of the abandoned child? What was she or he thinking?

These calls are never easy. Everyone else saw it coming, but the mother was the last to know. Her child has to suffer a huge loss and she's stunned from the double whammy. *How did I miss this?* she berates herself. *What am I supposed to tell my kids?*

When Janette gets home, she notices a card on the kitchen counter. ELLEN WINTER. OFFICE OF FRAUD DETECTION, FEDERAL COMMUNICATIONS COMMISSION. She turns the card over and reads, *Call me soon! Ellen.* She tacks the card to the bulletin board; if she doesn't remember why it's here in a few weeks, she'll stow it in the drawer with the other hundred pieces of paper she needs to deal with. Maybe when Spencer's off at Princeton she'll finally find the time.

When David gets back from Hawaii a few nights later, Janette asks him if he's working with anyone at the FCC. He gives her the what-are-you-talking-about look. David's the regular, jet-lagged kind of frequent flyer. Ask anyone who travels as much as he does: Reentries aren't easy. Trying to connect with your spouse, child, and life isn't easy when your brain's still in a heated eight-hour meeting in Honolulu. He prays there's no particular fire to put out right now.

"Did you leave this card here?" she asks. "Ellen Winter, Special Counsel?"

"What card? I don't know what you're talking about."

When Emma walks into the kitchen, she doesn't know anything about the card, either. Then she thinks for a moment. "*Now* I remember," she laughs. "That's the lady with the baby who chatted with me and Spencer at the Giant."

"Oh. Does she have a nanny?"

"As a matter of fact, she's looking."

Our investigative reporter looks straight at her husband the lawyer. "So let me get this straight," David says, glancing at the card. "She works in the Fraud Department at the FCC, but she has no qualms about poaching our nanny?"

"Don't worry." Emma laughs. "I'm not going anywhere. How could I leave my Spencer?"

But even if Emma weren't still content with her job—at least most of the time—the Huntington-Wilders have nothing to fear. First-time-mother Ellen Winter would probably faint from sticker shock if she knew Emma's salary.

20.

A NO-GOOD, VERY BAD DAY

J ANETTE HUNTINGTON has an uncanny ability to focus, to stay in the zone when it comes to high-stress situations. Does a reporter experience any other kind? The rest of the world is protesting our invasion of Iraq, the White House has withheld information from the Senate 9/11 Commission, and terrorists have bombed a Madrid train station. But the only story Janette gets to report today is that the President and Mrs. Bush have released their tax return.

A $2,000-a-plate Republican fund-raiser is another missed meal for Janette. She's on a perpetual diet anyway, fueled by her frantic pace. Not counting her recent thirty-six continuous hours with Spencer, Janette hasn't spent much time with him since he was born. Thank God her husband and nanny can carry on while she follows POTUS to the dreaded Crawford, Texas.

Janette's no spoiled network princess, and she keeps paying

her dues. When she asserts herself at a press conference the way the male reporters do, someone usually calls her pushy, or the B word. But she's used to it, and her audience share is up this week. A few of the more established correspondents resent rising stars, and it's a backstabbing industry. Reporters are always vying for top-dog status, and management likes it that way.

Some days, those soft stories turn into a lucky break. When the Easter Egg Roll on the South Lawn is rained out, Janette gets home an hour early to relieve her nanny, or was it her husband? She honestly can't remember if David's about to get on a plane or off one. He can hardly keep his meetings and timetable straight. It's Tuesday, so he must be in Hong Kong. Singapore. South Africa. If only he could outsource an extra brain, or, better yet, just clone himself.

When our road warrior finally gets home, he's eager to spend some fun time with his son. "I'll give Spencer his bath," David tells Emma, but then Dad's BlackBerry beeps again. After the water has gotten cold for the third time, Emma bathes Spencer herself and reads him a story.

David and Janette are always trying to reconnect with one another, too, since they're imaginary spouses most of the time. He's so involved in all the deals he's trying to put together, he's disoriented and detached when he's at home.

Janette doesn't complain about her job nearly as much as David does, but she's tired of watching the men get all the good stories. While her network nemesis is in Chicago giving a speech, she hears a leak—terrorists in Florida. She puts her notes in the hot file and calls New York to say she's on the story so they won't reassign it to Mr. First String.

She goes into high gear. *It's my story. I broke it.* The live shot she tapes on the North Lawn goes straight to prime time. During sweeps. Normally she wouldn't have even been in the lineup.

Serendipity. Right place, right time: the break Janette's been waiting for—and she was overdue.

Thank God for Emma. How many Very Important Women accept awards for their extraordinary accomplishments but forget to give credit to the nannies who've made it all possible? The smart, secure ones are grateful for the women standing behind them. Where would they be without their childcare?

Just like Winston Churchill, Spencer loves his parents from a distance and is thriving thanks to his nanny. Now that Janette's proven herself as prime-time material, she's even less involved at home. To the casual observer, the house looks clean and neat. The housekeeper stows the magazines and newspapers out of sight, but the stacks of unopened mail look more and more threatening. What bills aren't getting paid? What invitations aren't getting answered?

"Janette!" a neighbor says when they almost collide in front of Wagshal's. "Will we see you and David on Saturday?" How embarrassing. A Capitol Children's Academy board member, Carol Ferguson, just wrote Spencer's recommendation. *Oh, God. Can I pretend we never got the invitation?*

What about a new federal holiday: Read Your Mail Day?

Janette and David spend most of their rapid-fire conversations troubleshooting. Sometimes quarreling.

"Did you take my *Wall Street Journal* again?" she asks him.

"I can't spend my day off at the DMV. Can Emma get my Explorer inspected?"

"Emma has enough to do as it is."

When did Spencer get those new teeth? Is he really speaking in actual sentences? Mom and Dad are missing all the milestones.

"Did Spencer have his picture taken with the Easter bunny?" Emma asks. Janette and David look at each other. *Weren't you going to take him? You didn't remind me.* Spencer will be the only one in his playgroup who didn't get a basket of chocolate eggs.

One of my clients worked such long hours that her nanny was cracking from the strain. "Linda suddenly announced she's on overload," she told me. "She never complained before. What can I do *now?*"

My client was calling me from the hospital, where she was having a miscarriage.

In another memorable meltdown, a nanny called her boss to say she was leaving the children with a sales clerk at the Montgomery Mall Nordstrom. Whatever the last straw was, it had broken that nanny's back. "Come get your kids," she announced. "I can't do this anymore."

And then there was the nanny (not one of ours) who interrupted her physician employer *in the emergency room.* "You're late again," the nanny snarled. "I'm out of here."

"You can't leave now," the mother pleaded. "I have a patient dying on the table. I'm trying to put together a transplant team." She was paying this nanny $1,000 a week to watch her children fifty hours a week plus the occasional emergency, but the nanny left her in the lurch. Did she think there had already been too many emergencies? The children fended for themselves until the hospital sent a volunteer babysitter to the rescue.

Sooner or later, every working parent wants to split him or herself down the middle, and the Huntington-Wilders are no exception. *We have to figure this out,* they tell each other. When couples reach the tipping point, I'm the first to know, so I finally get the call

Janette and David didn't want to make. First the idle chitchat. Then, "It looks like we're going to need more help. Can we find someone for a few nights and weekends? We're maxing Emma out."

Even their sacred vow to travel only one at a time is no longer sacred. "I'll see who we have in our temp department to help you out on a regular basis," I tell David. "But I can't guarantee it'll always be the same person."

Now I have to put together a transplant team.

Even adding twenty hours a week to Emma's sixty, Janette and David won't be in our High Roller category. Believe it or not, I staff some families seven days a week. But it does give me pause, and I'm glad these parents can't see my raised eyebrows when they order 24/7/365 coverage. Outsourcing is fine when it comes to getting the groceries, dry cleaning, dog-walking, housekeeping, gardening, and the personal chef, but you can outsource your *parenting* only so much before things start to slide downhill fast.

That's when I ask myself the obvious question: *Why did they have these children?* Especially when a couple who are only barely managing *one* child decide to have a second—and a third. "We're having another baby," they announce with great excitement. When I hear this news about one of those *very* dysfunctional households (i.e., everyone needs psychiatric supervision, including the nanny), I can barely contain my horror until the call is over. "You're not going to believe this!" I shout. "The Samuelsons are having another baby!"

Then I hear a familiar chorus: *Oh-my-God-you've-got-to-be-kidding.*

But Janette and David only need a little bit of extra help—until Emma's father calls from England. Their nanny calls her mother once every few weeks, so the call's unusual enough to put Janette on high alert until it's over.

"Mum's in the hospital," Emma says, in a monotone. "She's having tests. My dad says I don't have to come home right now." Not wanting to talk about it, she disappears into her room.

Her employers, who both happen to be home at the same time, simply stare at one another. *If Emma leaves now, we're toast.*

"Can we ask her not to go right now?" David whispers.

"I can't say that to her, David. It's her *mother.* I'm in Iowa tomorrow. Can you call White House Nannies in the morning? *Please, don't forget this time.*"

"I didn't forget the last time. You forgot to tell me."

By the next morning, Emma has made her decision: Her family needs her.

"Emma's mother is in the hospital and it doesn't sound good," David says anxiously. "Now we need more than a little backup. Can you find us someone just as good?"

Now Janette and David's crisis is mine. Great live-in nannies aren't waiting around for clients to have emergencies. In fact, there's no one available now who's right for Wilton Road, so I'm in overdrive. My friends at the other local agencies don't have anyone, and neither do my friends in Boston and Atlanta.

Now I'm desperate.

And it's tax season, so I'm barraged by financial emergencies as well. "They haven't withheld my taxes," nannies tell me. "Now I owe the IRS as well as [take your pick] Maryland/Virginia/D.C. hundreds of dollars."

Most of *my* clients do everything by the book. If they're waiting for their next big government promotion, they won't jeopardize their careers by not paying household-employee taxes. But I'm no tax expert, so I outsource this job to one of the excellent companies who make sure these parents deal with the tax laws.

And in the middle of all this, why is my neighbor the ace personal injury lawyer calling me at work for the first time in fifteen years? We exchange pleasantries. "I've got a great nanny for you who needs a new job," he says. "Her name is Ashley Wells, and I know she'll be great. She's suing her former employer and I'm representing her."

The details of the lawsuit are sordid: Ashley's former employer was an Ivy League soccer dad with the despicable hobby of videotaping his nannies in the bedroom and the bathroom. Looking for a *Winnie the Pooh* tape, the nanny discovered her own name on one of the videos: TAMMY, 1999; KIMBERLEY, 2000; ASHLEY, 2002.

Washington parents, like vigilant parents everywhere, invest thousands of dollars in state-of-the-art cameras to make sure their nanny's doing a good job. Even though "nanny-camming" is a common practice, it always feels invasive, even when employers do it legally. Nannies must be told they're being taped, and cameras can only be installed where the nanny works (not in her bedroom or bathroom); audiotaping is forbidden.

Some clients place cameras all over their homes so they can watch their nanny and children whenever they want, right from their desks.

Now the nanny's feeding the baby applesauce. Now she's cleaning out the diaper pail. Such a fascinating distraction from the work Mom and Dad are supposed to be doing. (I'm surprised they're allowed.) And there's always the danger of misinterpreting what you see. For instance, if the nanny removes her blouse to wash the baby's spit-up off it, the parents wonder why she's walking around undressed in the middle of the day.

On the other hand, if your nannycam captures your baby's first steps, at least you'll get to see her do it. If you miss the live moment, you can always catch it on reruns.

I'm frequently asked my opinion about nannycams. Of course

parents have the right to make sure their children are safe. But when I hear "We're thinking of installing a camera," I can usually tell that the trust factor is gone. When a client has such nagging concerns that they're thinking about *surveillance,* I suggest they hire a different nanny. By the time they set up the cameras, they might as well be interviewing other candidates.

When clients want reassurance that their nanny's doing a great job, a surprise visit does the trick. It feels wonderful to see your caregiver doing a great job with your contented children, and that's what I suggested when a worried new mother called. "My baby is colicky, and I'm afraid my nanny will lose patience with her," she told me. "Actually, Barbara," she confessed, "I don't think she likes me *or* my baby very much."

This mother was right on one count. "The baby's getting easier," the nanny told me. *"But the mother isn't."*

"Why don't you drop in at home some afternoon?" I said. Surely that would allay the mother's fears. So she sneaked into her backyard and peeked in the window, and everything was fine.

But this client was the paranoid type and couldn't leave it at that. Next, she followed her nanny to the park, where she was easily spotted in her bright pink jacket, hiding in the bushes. The nanny felt completely undermined and was so mortified in front of her peers that she finally quit the job.

As I say all the time, trust is everything.

And next time, I'll tell that mother to wear camouflage gear.

My phone rings ominously again. Telephones don't always ring he same way, or maybe I'm just psychic. I'm afraid I'm on a downward slope today. "We adore Fatou, but she has to go back to Gambia," says one of my favorite young moms. "Her mother died and we're so sad for her. We'll need someone for about a month."

I tell her we'll get a temp to cover them. Then, as soon as I hang up, I realize this emergency sounds familiar. Didn't I console a nanny who lost her mother a few years ago—around the time I lost my own mother? *I have a sinking feeling that was Fatou.*

Even though there *are* cultural idiosyncracies, I'm pretty sure we all get just one mother.

I adore Fatou as much as her employer does, so now I'm really uncomfortable. I think I'll just let sleeping nannies lie.

Next, a British nanny calls, hysterical: Immigration sent her paperwork to the wrong address, so she wasn't able to renew her work permit before her deadline. "I can't even get an appointment to straighten all this out," she tells me. "I could be deported!" Ever since 9/11, the Immigration and Naturalization Service is totally backlogged, and a British nanny isn't high on their list of priorities. The nanny's employers are worried, too. But it turns out that the father works at the Justice Department, and he gets his nanny an immediate appointment.

We make absolutely sure our nannies are legal. No "Her papers are in progress" nonsense, or "You need to sponsor this nanny." I inherit a lot of disappointed clients who've been through those nightmares. But there can even be problems with entirely legal nannies. When a friend of a friend's Filipina nanny tried to renew her papers, she was actually handcuffed and held, incommunicado, in a Virginia Beach jail for two weeks. Luckily, her employer also had a congressional contact who helped spring his nanny from jail. Several years and thousands of dollars later, the wrongful decision was overturned.

Immigration tangles have never been simple. And these days, even my clients' connections don't always help.

I can't think straight anymore, so why do I make this final call of the day? A very highly placed Justice Department official and his attorney wife are moving back to California, and I need a reference so I can find their nanny a new job. When their twelve-year-old daughter tells me her parents aren't home, I innocently ask her what *she* thinks about her nanny.

"I spoke to your daughter," I tell the client when she calls me back ten minutes later.

"Yes, I know," she retorts icily. "You had no right to speak to her without my permission." Then I get a lecture about not talking to minors without parental permission—which of course I already knew.

Whoops. Time to get out of here before I break any more laws.

21.

SEARCHING FOR A MIRACLE

APRIL 2004
ADMINISTRATION RELEASES TOP-SECRET
  DOCUMENT
TORNADOES TEAR THROUGH MIDWEST
WHITE HOUSE CORRESPONDENT NEEDS
  NEW NANNY

"This couldn't be happening at a worse time," says hyperanxious Janette when she finds ten seconds to call me. "I finally got the promotion I've always wanted, and Emma had everything totally under control at home. Now I'll be traveling as much as David." She takes a deep breath and announces her news as seriously as a flood, a war, or a break in the Middle East quagmire. *"None of this will work without Emma."*

I've never heard her sound so on edge, and her anxiety is

catching. Janette's emergency is happening at a bad time for *me,* too, as a matter of fact. There are hardly any nannies looking for new jobs in April.

"Don't worry," I reassure her, as if I have a dozen great candidates ready to step in. "Just let me take on your stress."

"That sounds wonderful," Janette says, cheering up.

"That's what I do." And this time, I'm not kidding.

First, I get my temp department into gear. We have Sonia, a great live-in who has a free week coming up when her employers go on vacation, so she can probably pinch-hit. After that, maybe I can convince Ellie to fill in. She just retired from the nanny business to take care of her grandchildren, but she's available for short-term jobs. After that, someone permanent will come along—at least that's what I tell myself.

Live-in nannies are as rare as Democrats in the White House—any time of year. After I check my own pool of candidates, I go into high networking gear with other agencies around the country. As a former board member of the International Nanny Association, I have great contacts in every large city, so I immediately put out an all-points bulletin. *Helpppp!*

Ever since I sent Emma to Janette almost two years ago, our relationship has consisted of periodic check-ins and social niceties. That's how it usually is once my mission is accomplished. My dealings with clients are constant and intense at first, and then we drift apart, taking one another for granted. Kind of like marriage. If I've made the right placement, I may not talk to a client until she's pregnant again.

Or, in Janette's case, since her last nanny was.

When it's time to hire someone new, we're best friends again. And even if we haven't worked together for years, I can instantly retrieve the layout of the client's home, their nanny quarters, where her children go to school, and a hundred details about how she and her husband manage their complicated family's life. We talk several times a week, weighing the pros and cons of prospective nannies until they finally hire someone. Then we both move on.

At a Christmas party, I ran into a client for whom I found all five of her nannies. Betsy Valentine and I had only met face-to-face once, years ago, but after staffing her home for eight years straight, I know more about her than some of her best friends do. "How are Jenna, Christopher, and Max?" I asked Betsy. We both laughed at our instantly revived intimacy.

My friendship with ABC Correspondent Ann Compton grew stronger each time she needed a new nanny, too. After we met at the American University pool where our toddlers were learning to swim, she took a chance and hired me on the spot. After a few successful placements for Ann and her physician husband, I knew they preferred smart, energetic nannies and that they only expected each one to last a year or so. As the children grew, the job became more complex and entailed driving all four of them to different schools and all their other activities.

Ann was always a sheer pleasure to deal with: straightforward and appreciative of my efforts, as well as of each of her nannies' hard work. She needed total flexibility—i.e., night and weekend coverage so she could follow Presidents Reagan, Bush One, and Clinton until her children were old enough to take care of themselves.

Twenty years and eight nannies later, we're still friends.

I cherish these longstanding friendships. I still get to talk to one of my truly "vintage" nannies from Montana, circa 1988. Just when I think Toni's about to retire, she joins yet another family to start a new chapter of her childcare career.

And then there's Jamie, everyone's favorite nanny. (How many times have I said that about someone?) Her first job was taking care of a three-year-old and a baby for a couple who both worked *all* the time, sometimes out of the country. Jamie helped raise their three sons and was a true spouse to both parents for nine years.

Now that Janette's officially searching again, I e-mail her a new application for her updated information. The last time she filled one out, Spencer wasn't even born. What's her latest wish list? Do we need to find Emma's clone? (The White House Nannies Cloning Department is closed due to lack of government funding, so I sincerely hope not.)

Janette e-mails the application back, pronto: "Subject: We need a miracle! Traveling a LOT. I'll try to block out time to talk. Thanks for getting on this asap."

That gives me a few days to worry in peace about finding the nearly impossible: another Emma.

Finding the match for a family that has already had the ideal nanny is tough. But clients who've had positive experiences are so much easier to deal with than the ones who need to move on from a bad situation. Clients and nannies need to be fully informed about one another before they meet, so my policy is total disclosure. An interview isn't the right time for a surprise about incompatible faiths, diets, or lifestyles.

Latina as well as other third-world nannies are often reluctant to work for non-American mothers for fear of being treated as if they're back home, where class lines are still very clear. One client who requested a Spanish speaker was used to a full array of servants back home in Bogotá. During our interview, she was charming and engaging. But much to my surprise, every nanny I wanted to send her seemed to know more about that mother than I did. And *no one* wanted to work for her.

There are many grapevines in this town.

Filipina, Dominican, Brazilian, etc., nannies prefer to work in neighborhoods where they'll be able to socialize with other Filipinas, Dominicans, and Brazilians. (*Nannies of a feather . . .*) And then we have a globe's worth of specific requests: Sri Lankans would rather not work for families from India, for instance; and my down-home nannies from Minnesota aren't keen to work for families they consider too "exotic," which means anything other than American, white, and Lutheran, or maybe Catholic.

Another kind of hard sell, sometimes for good reasons, is childcare jobs where the mother works at home. A lot of my telecommuting clients have tried to work *and* take care of their children without help; then they realize that's too difficult— make that impossible—and call me.

"It was a nightmare," one journalist admitted. "It took seven days' worth of naps and my husband's limited time off to actually accomplish one day of work. Picture me carrying my son in the Baby Bjorn, desperately jiggling him up and down, holding the mute button on the phone so no one heard his bout of colic. I'd be typing with one hand while he slept on my lap and suddenly realize he'd peed through his clothes onto mine. Ugh."

But when these mothers finally hire help, they still find it hard to concentrate. The people on the other end of the phone may not realize the mother's at home, but every time she rushes down the hall to rescue her crying child, the nanny certainly knows where she is. Most nannies run the other way when I tell them a parent will be in the house, trying to work while they're with the children. They want to bond with the baby and be left alone to establish their own routine. When Mom or Dad is just down the hall, who do you think the child wants to be with?

"As soon as I got the baby calmed down and ready for his nap, my boss peeks in and he starts wailing again!" a nanny recently complained. "She can't leave her child alone. *Why did she hire me?*"

Dads who work at home, on the other hand, are mysteriously able to ignore their howling children—sometimes even when there's no nanny around to deal with them! Okay, make that *some* dads . . .

Let's fast-forward through a few difficult weeks in Janette's life as well as mine. Besides leaving no potential nanny unturned for her, I've been trying to help a few other desperate clients. One made the mistake of hiring a nanny *online*. "The minute she got off the plane, I knew I'd made a terrible mistake," she admitted. This mother has two small children and a job she's about to lose unless I find someone fast. Front burner.

And an attorney couple in a $3 million (so they told us) Georgetown home want me to, *please*, try again—after three nannies in a row have quit on them. No one wants to live in that house: rabbit poop everywhere, food from the last century in the fridge, moths in the cabinets, and mold in every corner. The last nanny swears she was on antibiotics for months after she moved out.

For obvious reasons, no one's crazy about the family, and each former nanny warns the next one, so she doesn't last for long. Yes, they have a housekeeper, but all she does is polish the silver. How do I tell someone, diplomatically, that their house is filthy?

"Can you call Mrs. X and give her the bad news?" I ask Karen sweetly.

"Are you sure you don't want to do that yourself?" she replies.

I go through every file I can think of and make a lot of calls to find Janette's new nanny. "We have to broaden our search," I've warned her. "I hope you don't have your heart set on the British Isles."

"I know," she said. "She won't be Emma." It's great to have a realistic client for once. When it comes to clients' wish lists, I definitely get some beauts. I'm always amazed when a client thinks they can custom-order a nanny as if she's a new car. And I quote: "We want someone intelligent, creative, with high energy to keep up with our active three-year-old. We like to expose the children to other cultures. We just got back from Africa, where we were living with pygmies."

Yes, you read that right. I wanted to say we were fresh out of pygmies, but that line's getting old. The client is a film producer and travels all over with his family. They live on an organic farm (where else?) when they're in the Washington area.

You'd think some clients were choosing an exotic vacation when they request a nanny. "Let's see, we've done Turkey. What about Greece? Or Italy?"

Why don't they just ask for a nanny from Mars or Pluto?

And whether they say it out loud or not, a lot of parents are *very* concerned about the *image* their nanny will project. (How silly of me to think it would be how she cares for their children.)

"She has to look good for the car-pool line."

"We travel a lot, and we want to be able to take her with us."

"I'd love an athletic nanny." (This is always code for *thin*.)

"Oh, one final thing I should mention . . ." I'm afraid of what's coming. "Of course *I* don't really care about this. But my husband really prefers a nanny who isn't overweight."

Should I ask for her husband's definition of "overweight"? This line sends me into orbit, and I can't let it slide. "You need to tell your husband the nanny's not his date," I inform the caller.

My hard work finally yields three possibilities for Janette and David, and they all look good, at least on paper: Adrienne, from Washington state, used to work for a single mom I always liked. The truth is, Adrienne was young and lacked the focus of a more experienced nanny, even though her job wasn't a difficult one. But that was six years ago, and her current references are stellar, so I hope that means she's matured.

A nanny agency owner in Boston sends me a package for Stephanie, who sounds smart and easygoing, the sporty type who'd have a lot of fun playing with Spencer when he's a little older. Stephanie's a good candidate, but she really prefers to stay in New England. She wouldn't know her way around Washington, and Janette and David will hardly have time to show her. Nannies need their support systems as much as the rest of us do, and since Stephanie has no friends in the area, she's not a good candidate for a job in Washington.

Eliana from Brazil has all the right qualifications, but when I talk to her on the phone I realize her language skills aren't very strong. Her references say she communicates well in person, but Janette and David won't see their nanny much, so that could be a problem.

Karen rushes in with a brainstorm for Wilton Road. "What about Rena?"

"Rena from Costa Rica? You're brilliant." She's a twenty-year career professional and definitely the take-charge type. The other good news about Rena is that she loves to cook. The employer she was with for four years reduced her to part-time hours and part-time pay, so she's anxious for a full-time position again.

Janette has the coded application.

I can feel it in my bones: Spencer's next nanny is only two phone calls away.

Make that a dozen. "Yes, I did say Rena could look for another job," says her boss. "But now that doesn't work for *me*, because I volunteer at the school library three mornings a week." I offer her the best temp nanny in the house, but no dice. She's going to be *really, really busy*. And besides, "Andy loves baking cookies with Rena."

What if I go over there and bake cookies with Andy myself?

"But your nanny will miss out on a fabulous full-time position," I tell her. Rena's not the type to disappoint an employer, even if that feeling isn't mutual.

"Rena absolutely cannot go. I *need* her."

Let's take a moment to discuss what "need" means. When a father in tears tells me he needs a nanny because his wife died giving birth to twins, that fits my definition of the word. When a National Guard dad has been taking care of three children while his wife works, and he has to leave for Iraq in two weeks, that family also *needs* a nanny.

I think I'll tell our volunteer librarian to look up the Emancipation Proclamation—when she isn't really, really busy.

Note to self: *Don't count your nannies before they hatch.*

22.

PASSION

EVEN THOUGH I GET TO WORK early these days, my desk is messier than usual. Don't ask what my house looks like. But there's no time to get organized; I have two nannies to interview. If none of them turns out to be Spencer's, I'll be working on sacred Wednesdays until I find her.

Emma calls, sounding anxious. "I'm so worried about Mum," she says, "I can't even focus on my job. You know how hard this is for me, but I'm going to have to go soon."

Two weeks to replace another Best Nanny in the World.

"Don't worry," I reassure Emma. "You're doing the right thing. We'll find someone great for Spencer." I hope I sound convincing. At least I have those temps up my sleeve, or I think I do.

I have a few minutes to reread the applications in my "Probably Not" pile, just in case I've overlooked a possibility for Janette. In her photograph, Marnie from New Jersey is wearing a T-shirt that reads ALL MEN ARE IDIOTS AND I MARRIED THE KING. *What was she thinking?* I show the picture to Karen. "Am I judging Marnie too harshly?" I ask.

"How's the rest of her paperwork?"

"About the same."

Karen gives me her enough-said look.

The next probably-not nanny's name is Blessing, and she's added a brief note to the bottom of her application: "I was raised Catholic but am presently in religious turmoil."

If *I* were Catholic, and if there were a patron saint of nannies, I'd be praying fervently to her right about now. And if I have to send Blessing to Janette, she won't be the only one in turmoil.

Blessing and Marnie graduate to Definitely Not, along with a nanny who begins the description of herself by telling me all about her narcolepsy. Fortunately, the phone distracts me. "You're going to love Isabella," says an agency owner in Atlanta. "She's perfect." Maybe, but Isabella wants to bring her fourteen-year-old daughter with her when she moves to Washington.

Back to the drawing board.

Adrienne greets me with open arms. We haven't seen each other in five years, but I remember her upbeat, positive disposition. *A little like Emma.* After she tells me about her last few jobs in California, I'm convinced her references are accurate: Adrienne does seem more grown-up. I'm starting to feel optimistic until she mentions she doesn't want a live-in job now because she's moved in with her boyfriend. *Not even if I beg?*

The next woman I meet has helped raise three children for the past seven years, and now they're all beyond the full-time-nanny stage. This is the inevitable course of events, but no one is ever prepared for the job they love to end. Many nannies in this situation are so overwrought they can barely talk. "I know how hard this is for you," I commiserate. "They're like your own children."

This is why I keep a box of Kleenex on hand. I don't know if senators cry when *they* leave office, but a woman who's spent years parenting someone else's children almost always leaves with a heavy heart. Do the math. Fifty hours a week times fifty weeks a year times five (on the average) years. She's spent 12,500 hours with your children, not counting all those extra nights and weekends. In fact, the end of a childcare position can feel like a divorce—except the nanny doesn't share custody of the children.

But many families maintain close relationships with their former nannies, and the children love visiting them on their ranches and farms in the heartland. Ann Compton's family keeps up with all eight of their former nannies, all over the country.

But even under the best circumstances, breaking up is always hard to do. When it's the nanny's choice, many parents are furious. "This is such a terrible time," they complain. Jeremy is having his bar mitzvah, or the family dog is having surgery, or the kitchen is being painted. The timing is always awful—unless it's *their* decision.

Like many Washington jobs, nannying occurs in what I think of as "terms." And when those terms are up, for a host of reasons, the caregivers I've known almost all feel as if they're being voted out of office. Whether you have a two-year House seat, a six-year one if you're a senator, or four or eight years if you live or only work in the White House, most D.C. jobs have predetermined conclusions. Remember what I said about our legendary revolving door?

In fact, our legislative elections can directly affect those nanny terms of office. Our constantly changing workforce and federal budget affect individual family finances and staffing as well.

"How much are you planning to pay the new nanny?" I asked a longstanding client with a highly visible husband. "I'll know on

November third," she said. "If the President loses, my husband will go into private practice." Where he'd make a lot more than he does now at his high-level government post.

I wonder who that nanny voted for.

This is what makes the Washington nanny business truly challenging. *If the Democrats/Republicans win we'll buy a bigger house. Or get a second nanny.* I also hear, *We won't need a nanny at all because I [or my husband] will be out of work. Or moving back to [fill-in-the-state].* This is how I get my constantly changing supply of new nannies to redistribute among my clientele.

Next, I meet a prospective live-out nanny named Yvonne and prepare her to interview with yet another pair of government attorneys. After discussing the hours and job description, I make sure Yvonne understands the difference between gross and net salaries and knows how to get to her interview so she'll be there on time.

We never script nannies, or "package" them in any way. Parents need to meet the unvarnished woman they'll trust with their children, so I never tell a nanny what to say or do during an interview. I do find out if she has CPR or first-aid training and how she drives. I get as many letters of reference as I can, and I always talk to her current or previous employers.

I make sure, however, that the nanny will present herself as a professional candidate. Some women need a bit of advice. If her thick cloud of perfume sends me gasping for air, or if she has blue nails or a nose ring, I might suggest a change or two.

Which I end up doing when I finally meet Eliana from Rio de Janeiro. Just as her employers mentioned, communication is easier with her in person than on the phone. But our all-important face-to-face meeting reveals another issue: I understand there's a great emphasis on *looks* in Brazil, but—where do I begin? It takes me a half hour to focus on the important part of our conversation, because the amount of cleavage Eliana has chosen to reveal is astonishing. Her lips are dramatically outlined, her eye makeup is theatrical, and her hair is gelled into Medusa-like ringlets.

Our Brazilian bombshell looks more like she's auditioning for a movie (perhaps X-rated?) than a childcare position. *Eye contact is really important here,* I remind myself, but I can't raise my eyes above neck level. "I just love babies," Eliana says. She literally oozes with affection. I know she means it, and I like her immensely.

We'll find Eliana a job, but not with Janette. Richard stops to say hello without even glancing at the candidate's décolletage. How nice to have a husband with his mind totally on business.

Karen and I, however, have to regroup when she leaves. Eliana will be fine, we both agree. "Don't worry, boss," Karen says. "I'll tell her to keep those tits under wraps from now on." Karen's Brit wit cuts right to the chase, as usual.

Now it's time for lunch, so I order my you-know-what-kind-of-sandwich and think about taking a trip to Brazil. Two ridiculous requests in a row interrupt my fantasy. "We have a very active little girl," says the next mother, "so we'd love an energetic nanny. You know, someone who can climb trees with our daughter."

I try to explain to this insistent, all-knowing executive, who's married to a senator, by the way, that her three-month-old won't be climbing trees for *years,* but she has no interest in my professional input.

"I know this sounds nitpicky," says a lawyer who heads up the summer internship program at her law firm, "but there are several errors in the nanny's application. Which is, quite frankly, Barbara, *off-putting.*"

I always laugh to myself when the parents of a *newborn* are concerned about a nanny's spelling and syntax. Since when does "i before e" have anything to do with how well someone cares for your baby?

The paperwork doesn't always tell the tale.

A t the very end of my day, I hear from Rena. I assume she wants me to commiserate with her about being held in bondage. I know she won't leave the children she loves when she's still needed, even if it means giving up a much better position. "Barbara, you won't believe what happened!" Rena sounds both aggravated and excited. *"Mrs. Johnson wants me to leave in a week!"*

After her four years of devoted, loyal service, I don't blame this nanny for feeling betrayed. Georgia Johnson expected two months' notice from Rena, but she's only giving *her* one week to find another job. And hardly any severance pay.

Rena's sentences are sprinkled with *Dios mío.* "I'm glad to get out of here for sure," she says. But I hear the sorrow in her voice. "I'm going to miss Andy and Carolina sooooo much." Then Rena reads my mind: "Is it too late to apply for that job taking care of a little boy?" she asks tentatively.

I practically shout with glee. "Rena, you're right on time!"

"My library schedule changed," reads Georgia Johnson's e-mail, "so we won't be needing Rena after all."

"Thanks for letting us know," is my terse response.

J anette's been sure all along that I'll pull the right nanny out of the universe for her, so she's been able to focus on oil spills and prescription-drug bills. She'll be in New York this week, but

David's home, and he's promised not to leave the country until his wife gets back—at least until they have a new full-time nanny in place.

But things are a little tense at home during Emma's final week. Spencer and his puppy are both *regressing.*

On a Sunday night, Emma and Charles, her boyfriend, insist on staying home with Spencer so David and Janette can go to a movie. The parents decide to meet at the Avalon near Chevy Chase Circle for the seven o'clock show. Janette arrives first and waits on line. David's the punctual type, so when he's fifteen minutes late, she starts to worry he won't get there at all.

What in the world—more specifically, Singapore, China, Japan, or South Africa—would prevent him from calling, or at least answering his phone? Who knows when they'll both have the same free night and a babysitter again after Emma's gone? Janette paces back and forth, imagining the various disasters that might have stolen her husband. People are filing into the theater and David's still nowhere in sight.

A vaguely familiar woman approaches Janette. Cindy—Cindy Turner? They know each other from a book club neither belongs to anymore. "So how are you, Janette? I haven't seen you in ages. You look great."

"Fine," she says, unable to even fake a smile. She looks at her watch again, ignoring Cindy, then mutters *where-the-fuck-is-he?* under her breath.

Whew! Where did that come from? Cindy makes believe she didn't hear a word. *Woman on the edge.* "Are you okay?" she asks.

"I'm fine," Janette answers in a not-fine tone of voice. (This is our smooth, beguiling correspondent?) Then, without censoring herself, something she's usually good at, a torrent of negativity rushes forth. "This was our first night out together in months and I have no idea where the hell my goddamned husband is."

She continues to unload on someone she barely knows until Cindy excuses herself with, "The movie's starting. Gotta go . . ."

David catches up with Janette as she's walking to her car.

"I know you're pissed," he says. "Just give me a chance before you blow up, okay?" She's speechless. "Let's bag the movie and get some dinner, Janette. We need to talk."

"*You* need to talk. Did your BlackBerry and your cell phone both break at the same time? I just humiliated myself in front of a total stranger. Do you have any idea how scary that is?"

They go to Arucola for a bottle of wine and some pasta. "They held me hostage until the contract was signed," David explains. "Six months of work almost went down the tubes at the last minute. I absolutely could not leave, even to go to the men's room." She knows how precarious those final pre-signing situations are: no communicating with the outside world. Not even to call the wife you're standing up.

David is almost forgiven, but he has more to say. "They want me to go back to China for a much longer trip. I can't believe I used to like the traveling." She waits for more, totally in the dark. "Look, Janette. I've gotten a few calls from the SEC. They're seriously courting me. One of us needs a sane, normal life. I've really been thinking about this. The truth is, the firm just isn't that important to me anymore. You and Spencer are."

"When did you figure all that out?" Janette's too surprised to realize she's already feeling a lot better. About everything.

"It took me a while, but the writing was on the wall. *We weren't working.* Even with Emma. They want me to handle international securities, which I'll actually enjoy."

"But why didn't you say anything?"

"I wanted to be sure. Look, Janette. You have a passion for what you do. I finally figured out *I don't*."

NEWSWOMAN LOSES IT

HUSBAND GIVES UP PARTNERSHIP

CAPITOL CHILD ACADEMY ACCEPTS SPENCER
    HUNTINGTON-WILDER

23.

FAMILY, CAREER, AND SANITY

I LEAVE A MESSAGE for Janette and David: "Good news. There's someone I'd like you to interview right away. I have a few backups, but my money's on Rena. She's a widow with grown children and looking for a new family. Let me know how it goes."

"Just shoot me if this doesn't work," I tell Karen after I hang up.

Finally relaxing in the den with Richard and Wally (Gillian's writing her college essay), I turn on the television. There's Janette's live shot on the North Lawn, filling us in on our nation's historic opportunity in Iraq to change the world. She's been up since what she calls dark-thirty, but a lead story on the morning news is worth a lot more to her than sleep.

You'd never know she's in dire childcare straits. The nanny who keeps her child happy and her career thriving is about to vanish without a successor in place. It's a dubious honor at this point, but I'm in on the secret. Thanks to Janette's makeup and hairstylists, trainer, and image consultant, and especially to the all-powerful tech crew she rewards constantly with doughnut holes and lattes, she looks fabulous.

I look like something Wally dragged in. But as one of the many standing behind those who are Up Front and Center, and making it all look so easy, I'm used to it.

Janette and David manage to get home by seven to interview my candidate together. Smart mothers make sure their husbands are on the hiring committee. ("If we make a mistake, he won't be able to blame me," one mother explained. *You were there. You could have asked about her boyfriend/pet rabbit/sleepwalking/inability to fry an egg . . .*)

Many first meetings between parents and nannies are awkward, but Janette and David put Rena at ease, and she feels welcome with them right away. Afterward, I listen carefully to Janette's report to make sure she's not glossing over any reservations because she's so anxious to hire someone right away. "David and I both think the chemistry's great with Rena," she assures me.

Things don't always go this well. Sometimes there are immediate fireworks—and I'm not talking about the good kind. I sent one frazzled think-tank mother a supercompetent nanny I was sure she'd like, but the match was a disaster. "I was trying to breastfeed my baby and she kept telling me I wasn't doing it right. Then she told me all the other things I was doing wrong with my colicky baby." It was the Clash of the Titans: The two of them couldn't agree about *anything,* except that they were *not* a match.

Determined to be wonderful parents, many of my clients read everything they can get their hands on about hiring childcare, and they solicit advice from all their equally informed friends. Some then fire questions at prospective nannies as if they're in court. Other parents spend the entire interview telling the nanny all about themselves and what they do, in far more detail than she needs to know.

"So, tell me a little bit about you," they remember to ask as they glance at their watches and realize it's time to wrap up. "When can you start?"

Some clients grill the candidate about who else has interviewed her, since the nanny-hire is yet another arena in which some Washington parents compete.

"Oh. Where do *they* live?" they ask not so innocently. Translation: *Do they have a larger house in a swankier neighborhood?*

"How many kids do they have? Oh, that's a much harder job."

And finally, to really kill off the competition: "How much are they paying? How many children did you say they have?"

The second interview is, hopefully, more relaxed—kind of like a play date. The parents usually leave the room so the nanny and their child can get to know each other. (When one set of nervous parents hid behind the couch, it only took their toddler twelve seconds to find them. Their six-year-old had greeted the prospective nanny by crushing a handful of Goldfish over her head. No wonder they were nervous.)

But Spencer takes to Rena right away. Since the feeling is clearly mutual, and the second visit goes well, she's offered the position. The new nanny then spends the rest of the day and the next one with Emma to learn the ropes. And then she's on her own, to add her warm, endearing style to the mix.

Most clients want a week or two of overlap so their current nanny can familiarize her successor with household routines. The person who really does the job seems like the logical one to do the training. Her log or journal of the daily schedule and other pertinent information are always useful for the new nanny. However, I strongly recommend a limited overlap, especially with small children, so the new caregiver can establish her own routines.

A child will usually cling to the nanny he or she already knows instead of bonding with someone else. When my clients realize that their child will feel conflicted spending time with both nannies, they know I'm right.

Even if the nanny's the one who decided to leave, she probably thinks that no one else can fill her shoes. She might drop a caustic hint to sabotage the new relationship. *What time did she tell you she'll be home? Don't count on it. She's never on time.* Families usually want to remain on good terms with their former nannies. But if she finds out that her replacement will be making more money than she did, she may never speak to the parents—or worse, the children—again.

When I suggest that parents train their new nanny themselves, they're always surprised at first. "This is your golden opportunity to change whatever routines aren't working as well as they could," I say. After I walk parents through this transition, they see the logic of my suggestions.

The parents I most enjoy working with know their nanny has the hardest job in the world, especially when they've tried to do that job themselves. Our nannies have rescued postpartum moms with severe depression, and they've held families together when parents are ill or absent.

I never forget to pay homage to these women who come to us with so many unexpected gifts. A mother called from California when she needed someone to watch her son at the hotel while she was in town for a meeting. She wanted to interview several candidates on the phone for this four-hour job. Twenty minutes and two thousand questions later, as he put it, my husband convinced this mother to let us make the choice for her.

When our temp, nanny Jane, called the mother to confirm the job, she asked if there was anything special she needed to know about the little boy.

"Well, yes," the mother said. "Alex needs to practice his violin."

"No problem," said Jane, "I'll bring mine." More karma. The client was thrilled to learn that her nanny for the evening just happened to play for the National Institutes of Health Chamber Orchestra.

I placed Melanie from Minnesota in several positions, starting in 1988. After she married and went to graduate school, Melanie and her husband eventually adopted three foster children whose mother had been addicted to crack. Sixteen years later, Melanie visited my office to show me a picture of her family. They were helping to build a house for Habitat for Humanity.

And speaking of unexpected gifts, I have to mention Jennifer. She first came to me when she was working at Talbot's, a waste of her true talents. While she had a college degree, Jennifer had no special training. But she did have the desire and the tenaciousness to devote herself to eight-year-old Caty and her brother Jackson, who lived down the street from me.

Specialists had given Caty's parents the devastating news that she had Angelman's Syndrome and would never walk or talk. Caty's parents were determined to move mountains to help their child. And so was Jennifer, who spent hours every day on tedious, repetitive tasks, refusing to give up on Caty.

"Barbara, come here!" my husband shouted at me one Saturday, six months later. "You won't believe this." There was Caty, taking halting steps in her leg braces while Jennifer held her hand.

Our nannies have ridden on Air Force Two, attended White House events, and traveled all over the world with wonderful and sometimes famous families. Many of these women have used their placements as springboards to other careers and families of their own.

Some of them now employ their very own White House Nannies.

I love what I do. I've highlighted the funnier exceptions, but most of my placements turn out to be fine and long-lasting matches. I enjoy the constantly changing cast of characters—the brand-new moms and dads as well as all my recurring players.

The best way to get through child-rearing dilemmas is with a large dose of humor. When things weren't so funny in our house, I looked for a psychologist to help my young family with our growing pains. The woman I found had three children of her own and admitted going through some of the same craziness we were experiencing. She taught me to see the best in my children when parenting felt overwhelming. And ever since, because she knows I've been there, too, she's referred her patients to me for their childcare.

Family, career, and sanity. Who doesn't want to win this Triple Crown, even though the new human being in the house often seems determined to derail us?

The baby's interrupting our life!

I listen to parents describe all kinds of scenarios. Some sound like astonishing circus acts, no less treacherous than being shot out of a cannon or walking the high wire. Having a child is thrilling, but how are we supposed to keep everything else— work, relationships, our bodies, and our golf games—*on track*?

The answer is, you really can't—at least not the way you're used to. Not even the best nanny SWAT team can replace what children and parents need most of all: one another. But with the right attitude, sanity's within your grasp—especially if you find truly gifted caregivers to help out.

My theory is the ancient Chinese one: everything in balance.

More good news: The crazy early parenting years are the best ones—at least when you look at your old videos. Among our child-rearing challenges, Richard and I have dealt with ear infections, sensory-integration and attention-deficit issues, sibling rivalry, mean middle-school girls, wrestling and lacrosse defeats, and college applications. We've hired babysitters, nannies, occupational and speech therapists, and a plethora of tutors. We've had adventures with the law.

We've even dealt with our miniature schnauzer's canine cognitive dysfunction—which is kind of like Alzheimer's for dogs— and with Willy's subsequent death. The rest of the family, especially his brother, Wally, still miss him.

But lo and behold, my family has evolved into four independent adults. Okay, make that *almost* independent. And *almost* adult. During our children's exhausting early years, Richard and I often couldn't wait to escape the tedium. Who knew Matt and Gillian would become such great company? These days we can't wait to be with them.

My clients have just begun the long, wild ride—in this pressure-cooker Capital of Spin. Washington is a relentlessly competitive place where people parlay their contacts and bet on the right party in order to cultivate—or become—the next rising star. The parents I know are determined to enjoy the lives they've worked so hard to create, and I enjoy helping them get there.

So here's to David Wilder, who chose sanity and family over an overrated senior partnership. No one asked him to do it— certainly not his wife. "I finally figured out what success is," he told me. "It's knowing I can get home every night by six-thirty—

okay, sometimes it's more like seven—and hang out with Spencer. I can even spend time with Janette when she's around."

It took a while for the realization to grab hold of him and not let go. In fact, David got his best idea from Washington itself. It came to him during the daily runs he takes to clear his head. He follows the Potomac River from Haines Point past the Jefferson Memorial all the way to the Lincoln Memorial. It's a majestic route any day of the year, inspiring enough to put things in perspective.

If I can be trusted to predict this family's future, Janette and David will soon feel better knowing they're *not* dependent on any one person—even their nanny. David's mother will be thrilled that her son, daughter-in-law, and grandson are eating Rena's home-cooked meals. And Spencer will learn a little Spanish.

And, since I suspect his parents don't really want him to be an only child, I've made sure Rena knows about that possibility.

It's typical. As soon as everything's under control again, they'll add another daredevil act to their circus.

That's what keeps me in business.

BARBARA'S TIPS FOR FINDING THE PERFECT NANNY

Trust your instincts. If you can't get past a prospective nanny's nose ring and tattoo, hold out for someone else.

•

Call all references yourself. Some parents "forget" to tell an agency things they'll share with another parent.

•

If an agency costs less, it probably doesn't spend enough time making sure its nannies are well qualified.

•

When both parents interview a prospective nanny, it's no one's fault if the relationship happens to go south.

•

An "overlap" should be long enough for your old nanny to show her successor the ropes—but not long enough for them to bond, in case Old Nanny tells New Nanny something you wish she hadn't

·

Don't expect your nanny to devote nine of her ten hours a day to developmentally appropriate play with your children.

·

Don't give your nanny mixed messages. If you tell her she can have her boyfriend over, don't look surprised when he shows up.

·

Call an agency yourself. Even if you have a Chief of Staff, don't outsource this particular hire.

·

Don't micromanage your nanny. If you're calling her a dozen times a day, quit your job and take over hers.

·

Tell your nanny and your children your *real* schedule—not the one you wish you had.

·

Repeat this mantra at least once a day: My nanny's job is harder than mine.

·

Career. Family. Sanity. When life get difficult, just pick two out of three.

Acknowledgments

It took a great team to get *White House Nannies* launched. After I had threatened to write a book for so many years, one day my husband handed me a brochure from the Writer's Center in Bethesda, Maryland, and said "Sign up and start writing." It was there that I learned about Jeff Kleinman of Graybill & English whom I hounded until he agreed to be my agent. He is an exacting taskmaster, a savvy, smart guy. When he was so overwhelmed with a big project, he brought on Kristen Auclair who has been a superb co-agent. She is a great editor, sounding board, and the right demographic (a new mom!).

I am also most grateful to the very professional team at Jeremy P. Tarcher/Penguin. I will forever be thankful to my wonderful editor, Sara Carder, who championed the book, her helpful assistant, Ashley Shelby, and my very kind copy editor, Stuart Calderwood. Many thanks also to Tarcher publisher Joel Fotinos and fabulous Tarcher publicists Ken Siman and Kat Kimball.

This book would not have happened without Jill Teitelman, who is a gifted writer and editor. She took my words and made them flow. What a great team we were—from Nantucket to Brewster Park, from Boston to Washington, we slogged through twenty years of stories stored in my cobwebby brain. While creative and funny, she always strove for perfection. We fretted through deadlines, the worst of which involved our children's college early-decision applications. We rejoiced with their acceptances and with finshing the book early. It has been a great year working together.

Special thanks to Jeff Goldman, Sheila Conlin, Pam and Allison Sheff, Roger Sherman, Gianna Allentuck, and Jaime Wales for their valuable insights. To Shelley Robinson who helped with the final editing. To Kiki McLean, for knowing everyone in D.C. and being willing to call them. To my past and present team at the White House Nannies office: Karen Digby, Victoria Sciulli, Liz Stone, Margaret Auger, Mary Kay Lydanne, Jeniffer Greene-Hawkings, Karen Wilson Shaeffer. Also to my Washington friends who stumbled laughing and crying through their child-rearing years with us: Joanne and Scott, Shelley and Steve, Doreen and Michael. To my sister, Sallie Stern, who is my book reviewer, movie previewer, partner in laughter and tears. And, of course, my long-suffering husband, father extraordinaire, who always supports me in any and every thing I do. In stark contrast to other spouses who get acknowledged for their hours of input into a book's development, mine never read a single word I wrote—by design. His determination to mitigate matrimonial strife was admirable—in retrospect. And to Matt and Gillian who know they are more likely to be roasted than toasted—please know that without you two I wouldn't be half as smart.